The TWELVE ABSOLUTES
— of —
LEADERSHIP

GARY BURNISON

New York   Chicago   San Francisco   Lisbon   London   Madrid   Mexico City
Milan   New Delhi   San Juan   Seoul   Singapore   Sydney   Toronto

The *McGraw·Hill* Companies

1 2 3 4 5 6 7 8 9 10   DOC/DOC   1 9 8 7 6 5 4 3 2

ISBN   978-0-07-178712-3
MHID 0-07-178712-7

e-ISBN   978-0-07-178676-8
e-MHID 0-07-178676-7

Library of Congress Cataloging-in-Publication Data

Burnison, Gary
      The twelve absolutes of leadership / by Gary Burnison.
        p. cm.
      ISBN-13: 978-0-07-178712-3 (alk. paper)
      ISBN-10: 0-07-178712-7 (alk. paper)
      1. Leadership. I. Title. II. Title: The twelve absolutes of leadership.
      HD57.7.B8667 2012
      658.4'092–dc23   2011044708

McGraw-Hill books are available at special quantity discounts to use as premiums and sales promotions or for use in corporate training programs. To contact a representative, please e-mail us at bulksales@mcgraw-hill.com.

This book is printed on acid-free paper.

Knowledge is what you know,
wisdom is acknowledging what you don't know.

To all leaders everywhere, it's never about you,
but it starts with you.

ACKNOWLEDGMENTS

I wish to express with my deepest appreciation to the distinguished leaders who shared their wisdom, experiences, and stories to illustrate the absolutes of leadership: Angela Ahrendts, Warren Bennis, Sally Blount, William Clay Ford Jr., Peter Guber, Daniel Lamarre, Vineet Nayar, Kevin Plank, Mark Thompson, Ali Velshi, and Jeff Weiner.

I extend my thanks to my dedicated colleagues at Korn/Ferry, for the contributions they make each day to our clients and all those whom we have a privilege to serve.

My gratitude goes to those who helped secure interviews for this book, including Ken Whipple, Joel Kurtzman, Bill Simon, Bob Damon, Don Spetner, and Vanni Treves. I also wish to acknowledge our team, including Michael Distefano, Dan Gugler, Dana Martin Polk, and Tricia Crisafulli, as well as my colleagues at Lominger.

Special thanks go to our publisher, McGraw-Hill, and our editor, Mary Glenn, for her support and enthusiasm for this project.

Last, but by no means least, I wish to acknowledge my family: my wife, Leslie, and my children, Allison, Emily, Jack, Olivia, and Stephanie, who remind me every day that it is not what I do, but who I am, that matters.

CONTENTS

INTRODUCTION

Essential Links in the Leadership Chain

L eadership is the eighth wonder of the world—better seen and felt than defined and said. It's easy to intellectualize, but elusive to actualize. Leadership is part strategy, but mostly judgment. Always it is about grace, confidence, and touch.

I describe the responsibilities of leadership as being "all in, all the time," as in a high-stakes card game in Macao, in which you must double down every hand. There are no half measures when it comes to leading others. You must be fully engaged and fully committed, but you must never personalize what is happening around you or even to you.

As the leader, you must be cognizant of the past, intensely focused on the present, and constantly scanning the horizon for what the future will bring. Your starting point is the here and now, the results that you realize today. From here, you must execute a strategy to take you *there*—a point that your team members may or may not be able to see as yet. As the leader, you paint the outline, allowing others to collaboratively fill in the canvas.

So how does a leader accomplish all that? The answer lies in these pages. *The Twelve Absolutes of Leadership* provides you with the essential ingredients for extraordinary leadership. Think of these elements, as illustrated in the framework in Fig. I-1, as the links in the leadership chain, each one connected to the one before and morphing into the one that follows. These links represent both competencies and activities that all leaders must possess and master, regardless of their leadership style.

Figure I-1 The Absolutes of Leadership Framework

The first "absolute" is lead, the mission and aspiration for every person who is called to influence others. Being a leader is not about a title, salary, or privilege. It is being responsible to and for others, from the livelihood of your employees to the expectations of key stakeholders. To lead is to be all in, transparent and accessible, calm in the face of upset and even crisis, and always mindful that you are a steward of something bigger than yourself.

The journey to leading starts with the next six elements of the framework: purpose, strategy, people, measure, empower, and reward. Every organization starts with a vision and a purpose—the "what" and the "why" of its existence. Then comes strategy, the "how" and, more subtly, the "when" of its game plan to realize that purpose. People are the truly essential element, embracing the purpose and executing the strategy. Measure determines the progress the organization is making—what is working and what is not. Empower means to delegate to people, not just as individual performers, but as teams aligned with the purpose and strategy. Reward is celebration, not just compensation.

In addition, there are five more links, activities in which a leader must be constantly engaged. Although we define them separately here, they operate concurrently and in every phase of leadership. They are anticipate, to determine what tomorrow is likely to hold; navigate, to adjust and correct your course in real time to address opportunities and obstacles; communicate, to provide information and inspiration; listen, gathering feedback and intelligence from all sources; and learn, which must be a lifelong passion for every leader.

Despite all the frameworks and models that exist, leadership is much more art than science. It can be learned and absorbed only by doing, starting with the most important lesson of all: self-mastery. To lead is to manage yourself first, understanding that is it never about you, even though you may be in the spotlight more often than not, and uncomfortably at times. During good times, you will get more credit than you deserve, and during difficult periods, you will shoulder most of the blame and the burden. Even when you are tempted to take it personally, don't. You cannot be obsessed with the critics or with the yes people who jump on your bandwagon.

At its best, leadership is a vocation, a calling. It is a heavy responsibility that far outweighs the privileges, calling to mind the words that from those to whom much is given, much is expected. At the heart of it, leadership is how you make others feel.

It is my hope that *The Twelve Absolutes of Leadership* will define your leadership path—a journey that is about enabling others by discovering yourself, as you commit yourself to being all in, all the time.

CHAPTER 1

LEAD

*Do not go where the path may lead,
go instead where there is no path and
leave a trail.*

— *Ralph Waldo Emerson*

y the time you reach the level of senior leader, you have already mastered the technical skills that you need. What you may be missing, however, are the nuances and the seemingly simple truths that get lost in all the noise around how to run an organization. More often than not, a leader's blind spots stem from a lack of these softer skills, which may look very simple, but are deceptively so. There is nothing simple about empowering people so that the decisions they make and the actions they take are in line with the overall values and strategy of the organization. It is not easy to reward your team continuously with praise and acknowledgment of milestones achieved, particularly when you must steer a supertanker of an organization toward an endpoint that is over the horizon.

Leading is less about analytics and decisions, and much more about aligning, motivating, and empowering others to make those decisions. Leading is learning from the past to define the future, inspiring others to move purposefully forward. To lead is to acknowledge the reality of the here and now, while always focusing on tomorrow.

Being a leader, being a CEO, is not just a position; it's a lifestyle choice. It consumes you well beyond the hours and the travel. Inevitably, "work/life" will not always be balanced. The mental and emotional energy required is far more than you'll realize until you're actually in the CEO role. The obvious, but elusive "making others believe" requires you to be "all in." Authenticity will always trump charisma. I have found that the best source of authenticity is belief—that is, your own belief in the organization's mission. To convey that "everything will be okay," the sense that together the team will punch through a small opening in the sky, means allowing others to look into your eyes and see your soul. You must believe.

The lessons from the leadership journey are numerous. I am continually reminded that I'm not simply a messenger of our strategy. I am the message—not only in words, but in demeanor, mannerisms, decisions, behavior, and actions.

Make sure you have a hand on the wheel. Leadership is a contact sport. Read and interpret "between the lines." Empower others, but venture out yourself to listen and learn, to separate perception from re-

> *Go as far as you can see;*
> *when you get there, you'll*
> *be able to see farther.*
> — *J. P. Morgan*

ality. Have lofty thoughts, but be grounded, too. Separate what you do from who you are, all the while keeping heroic aspirations and recognizing that leadership, like life, is a journey.

Anchor Yourself in Humility

As a leader, you must have confidence in your own ability and, more important, in your team. But you must never cross the line into cockiness. Often it is a fine line, particularly when you are rallying your team members, helping them to see what is possible and what is within reach. With humility, you are reminded of where you came from and that the future is not guaranteed. You must relentlessly drive performance.

> Leaders are mirrors for the entire organization.

Humility is not about demeaning yourself, shrugging off your accomplishments, or downplaying yourself in any way. Humility means that you know who you are, where you've been, and what you have accomplished to get where you are. With that knowledge, you *can* get out of your own way and focus on others with the confidence that you can lead, inspire, and guide people—that you can help them to do and become more than their own vision for themselves.

To be a leader is not to compete with anyone else, whether it's your predecessor, a peer, or a role model. You've got to play your own game. I learned this lesson years ago when I played competitive golf. When you're on the course, you don't think about the other players or the gallery watching you. Your focus has to be 100 percent on what matters most, which is the shot you're about to take. The same is true for leaders, who cannot afford to be distracted by outside forces that allow one's ego to get involved. What matters most is the organization—where it is headed and the team's ability to get it there. That's the game that's being played, here and now.

Leadership is taxing and burdensome. It's not the visible stuff—the long hours, travel, pressure, and responsibility. Yes, leadership means working hard—being the first one in and the last one out; going to bed and waking up caring about the organization and its employees. But it's also what goes on behind the scenes that consumes so much emotional energy. You serve as the mirror for everyone else, reflecting optimism and confidence.

Leaders are mirrors for the entire organization. If they are down, the organization will follow. If they reflect brightness, the organization will shine. Leadership is making certain that after every conversation with an employee, the person feels better, more capable, and more willing to stretch than before the conversation began.

> *It is better to lead from behind and to put others in front, especially when you celebrate victory when nice things occur. You take the front line when there is danger. Then people will appreciate your leadership.*
> —*Nelson Mandela*

o   Balance heroics with humility.

o   Humility is the grace that constantly whispers, "This is not about you."

o   If it is done with sincerity, leadership should be humbling. Your leadership will shine the spotlight on others and what they achieve.

o   Leadership is a privilege and a responsibility, not an automatic right. Others must stand on your shoulders.

o   Past performance doesn't guarantee future success.
     Eschew entitlement. As a leader, you have to earn the
     right to your title every day.

For the Leader, There's No Such Thing
as Having a Bad Day

Being a leader means that you don't have the same freedom
you once had. Until you have the title, you don't fully com-
prehend the "all-in" intensity required to be the leader with
the final say—what it takes to be CEO. This is the emotional,
spiritual part of leadership that you can't learn from anyone
else. You can observe it, but you cannot truly experience it
until this opportunity and burden are on your shoulders. Only
then can you know what it's like to be "on" 24/7.

When I was an operating officer, I was "one of the guys."
People viewed me as a person, not as a function, which meant
that they spoke their minds to me. Receiving unfiltered feedback was never a problem. Because people viewed me as
"Gary," not as a position, I was even allowed to have a bad day
once in a while without its affecting the company. That all
changed when I became *the* leader.

Five years ago, I became CEO of Korn/Ferry, a New York
Stock Exchange–traded company operating in 40 countries
around the world, and the world's largest executive recruiting
firm and a leading global provider of talent management solutions. With this position came the responsibility for growth
through the "care" of our customers and the "feeding" of
our employees, as well as the ultimate accountability to our

shareholders for performance. At that point, leadership became all-consuming.

By the time I became CEO, I had presumably developed the requisite technical skills—the ability to strategize, implement, and execute. And I thought I had mastered the soft skills—the ability to shift from individual accomplishment to team performance, from what I do to enabling others to do. But suddenly, I was no longer just myself; I represented the position and, more important, the institution. I noticed that the people around me began reading my mood like tea leaves. Such a change can be disconcerting for any person, but for a leader, it cannot result in isolation.

> Leadership is grace, dignity, and restraint.

When I was first promoted to CEO, on several occasions—whether I was in a meeting, giving a speech, or having a phone conversation—people would ask me, "Are you okay?" At first I couldn't figure it out. Then it dawned on me. I had failed to appreciate that equally as important as what I was saying (and perhaps even more important) was how I was saying it. From that moment on, I shifted. I did away with PowerPoints, and I made sure I focused as much on my tone, my attitude, and the energy with which I spoke to and interacted with others as I did on what I had to tell them.

I could not just talk about the mission; I had to exude a steadfast belief in it. No matter how worried I might be about the economy, the stock market, competitive pressures, or a dozen other things, I couldn't show it. My burdens were mine alone. It didn't matter that everyone else's burdens were also mine; it was my job to keep my worries, concerns, and problems to myself.

As the leader, you cannot allow your gray days to show. If you do, others' perceptions of what you're thinking or feeling will become their reality. Pessimism and doubt are simply not an option. No matter what worries or concerns are on your mind, you are always the one who people look to for direction and assurance. Your team needs to know that "we're going to get there," and that a game plan exists to make that belief a reality, particularly when things are not going your way.

Leaders are in the confidence-building business. As the CEO, I was responsible for developing and projecting confidence. Such confidence was not about me personally, but it needed to be *in* others and the organization, with assuredness of the vision, the journey, the team, and what we could accomplish together. The global financial crisis of 2008–2009 brought this point home to me in a powerful way. We had achieved revenue and profitability levels that set records for the company's 40-year history. Shortly after the collapse of Lehman Brothers in late 2008, however, our industry, like almost every business in the world, experienced a white-knuckle free fall. Clients retrenched, and some global companies went out of business. Cash became king. Our organization was a microcosm of the global economy: we saw a multi-hundred-million-dollar loss of revenue over days.

In the surrounding chaos, we decided to orient our organization toward opportunity, not crisis. This isn't to say that we didn't have to make difficult decisions. We did, but we made these choices immediately and navigated decisively. This is because we had anticipated the problem well in advance, although obviously not the depth of the crisis or the near-collapse of the banking system. However, I had said publicly in September 2007 that an economic downturn was coming. In the ensuing months, we had prepared a contingency plan anchored around opportunity and confidence—preserving the brand and as many jobs as possible, and, equally important, positioning the company for growth as we accelerated out of the economic downturn. When the recession hit, we were ready. We moved the organization from uncertainty to certainty. Even though we asked our employees for personal sacrifices (such as furloughs and pay cuts), we established a tone of confidence in the operating plan, in the destination to which that plan would lead us, and, most important, in our people.

> *Lead, follow, or get out of the way.*
>
> —*Thomas Paine*

During the crisis, Korn/Ferry completed three strategic acquisitions, launched online and offline marketing initiatives, and added employees in strategic markets, which enabled us to significantly expand our talent management business worldwide. The result has been postrecession growth that has substantially outpaced that of the competition. My confidence in making such moves came from knowing the capability of the people in our organization as well as anticipating a better future. We had saved during the better times so that we would be able to invest during a period of crisis. I have come to appreciate how organizations can make their best strategic, cultural, and operational moves during difficult times.

- o   To lead is to give, not to receive.
- o   Seek commonalities among people, not differences. By embracing commonalities, uniqueness can be celebrated.
- o   Immediately redirect conflict into positive action.

It's Lonely at the Top, but Don't Make It Isolating

The first challenge for any leader is to take charge. Yes, you have a leadership team and several close confidants. But unlike every other job you've had, where there was someone above you making the final decision or having the last word, you're *it*. Taking charge doesn't mean telling people what to do or what to think, but rather telling them what to think about—in other words, the why as well as your intent, which will have to be carried out many times over. Taking charge also entails finding the balance—mastering the yin and yang of leadership; knowing when to shift between pushing and pulling the team and the organization. For any leader, taking charge means that you don't run things on the basis of consensus or committee. Leadership requires making crisp decisions and explaining your intent so that others can carry it out.

Taking charge requires focus. As the CEO, you have the luxury of knowing that if you don't like something, you can change it. You don't have to accept the explanation that "that's how we've always done things" or "that's just the way it is." The bad news, however, is that changing anything requires time, energy, and resources. So while leadership is not laissez-faire, it is also not change for the sake of change. A great leadership team continually monitors whether it is focused and involved in the real game changers.

Taking charge means setting not only the strategic agenda, but also the length and pace of the runway needed to actualize that agenda. The CEO of a large U.S. company is in the job for an average of five years. Some departures are planned; others are not. The job can be taken away from you at any time; it's not a lifetime appointment. This is why your focus has to be on momentum changers. As the leader, you must recognize that the endpoint of your leadership term is not the endpoint of the organization. You are part of a leadership continuum. Just as you took over from someone else, so a successor will eventually follow you. Your job, therefore, is to be a source of energy and change to grow the organization, as well as to be a steward during the time of your leadership. Your goal should be to elevate and improve the organization and then turn it over to another leader in better shape than it was when you inherited it.

> The accountability you want to see at every level must start with you.

The leadership experience can only be described as a humbling privilege. Yes, there are extrinsic rewards that come with having the corner office with a view, but these are clearly secondary. To stand before the team as the leader—to shine the spotlight on its members and their accomplishments, and to feel that we are truly all in this together—is an indescribable feeling. To lead is to earn the trust of others, to know that when you climb the next mountain, others will be with you.

When you reach the top of the proverbial pyramid, you quickly realize that nobody else is there. You are the one in charge; it's all on your shoulders. The danger is that you can become insulated—even isolated. If you are out of touch, it's easy to get sidetracked by the layers and layers of other constituencies: media, special-interest groups, the critics, the "yes" people, even stockholders. Keep a laser focus on those who matter most: employees and customers. Although others may have a say in your approval rating, these two groups determine your ultimate performance.

To keep from being isolated, stay connected to your close advisors who are able to give you honest feedback, particularly about yourself. Take it as a fact: when most people look at you, they do not see you as a person; you represent the company. When you speak, be measured—your words will be taken literally. They no longer represent your own position; they are the voice of the institution. Only the outliers around you will behave differently. These are the rare people who will tell you things as they really are, who have the courage to give you the "bad news" instead of just telling you what they think you want to hear.

For most people, though, there is no real "freedom of speech" where the leader is concerned because they don't have economic freedom—meaning that they'll always think about their paychecks first. Try to reduce these tendencies. Create a safe environment, with no retribution for people who deliver bad news. Ask questions, listen and learn, and decide—not judge. But don't be naïve; people's desire to sugarcoat and put a spin on things will never be truly eliminated.

Most important, rely on those who remind you that you are not your job, such as your spouse, family, and close friends. Create social outlets for yourself outside of your professional capacity. Maintain a balanced perspective that keeps you in touch with people who know you as a person, not as a job title.

Know that, as a leader, you will get too much credit when things go well and too much blame in bad times. The sign on Harry Truman's desk said it best: "The buck stops here." As the leader, you are responsible—not only for making the final decisions, but also for the consequences of those decisions. As I began working on this book, I was reminded of this in a conversation with my surgeon while having a minor procedure done. When the surgeon asked me what I did for a living and I explained, his response floored me: "I could never do what you do. That's too much responsibility." Here was someone who, in my view, has direct influence over a person's health and well-being, and yet he saw being a CEO as too great a burden. The point is that to be a leader is to be responsible. If something goes wrong, it doesn't matter whose fault it actually is; it's up to the leader to take responsibility. If a person is going to take the title, he has to be comfortable with all the implications that come with it.

Being responsible means being decisive based on the best information at hand, which may be incomplete or subject to change. You won't always be right; no one ever is. Whatever the outcome may be, you need to live with it. But as a leader, you cannot let things drift. You must deal directly with situations in the midst of ambiguity and uncertainty. Leadership can't wait for clarity. It is about making and seizing opportunity—not by sitting paralyzed by pundits or enamored by glad-handers, but rather by going out and listening to and learning from those who matter most: customers and employees.

Responsibility, however, is much more than the obvious "it happened on my watch." It is as much in the subtle messaging. Take responsibility for modeling behavior for the organization—the so-called walk the talk. At every opportunity, I speak with employees about our company's heritage, purpose, culture, and values. Furthermore, as a leader, if you turn a blind eye to or allow behavior that is inconsistent with your stated words on values, people will simply stop listening. Your words will be meaningless. Behavior or value judgments, which usually are "tough people calls," must be made swiftly, but discreetly, with dignity and due process. How these situations are handled is as important as the decisions themselves. In other words, people will look at the way others are treated and wonder whether that is the way the organization will treat them. I have found that these decisions, more than any other, ripple through the organization like a pebble in a pond.

> Words motivate, actions inspire.

Similarly, if a bad fit or a problem employee is not dealt with expeditiously, the situation becomes a cancer in the organization. I recall a situation in which an employee did something that was not illegal, but was clearly unethical as a business practice. What made this situation a bit tricky was the fact that our firm didn't have a written policy covering this practice. Therefore, it could conceivably have been rationalized or explained away, especially since the employee in question was a top performer. In my mind, however, there was no doubt: the action was clearly wrong and could not be tolerated. As a consequence, I terminated his employment.

A few weeks later another employee in a different city, who was also a top performer, called me aside. "You know, if you hadn't fired him," this employee told me, "I would have quit. I would have questioned what we stand for as an organization."

The moral of this story is that, as the leader, I am ultimately responsible for what happens in the firm. If someone acts unethically on my watch, it is up to me to step up to the challenge of doing something about it.

> *Being prime minister is a lonely job. . . . You cannot lead from the crowd.*
>
> *—Margaret Thatcher*

When challenges arise, leaders can't engage in the blame game, saying, "It was someone else's fault or responsibility— not mine. I'm the CEO; how can I know everything that is going on?" As soon as the people on your team hear those words or observe that behavior from you, they will immediately go on the defensive and wonder whether they will be blamed when something goes wrong in the future. They'll clam up on whatever feedback they're giving and, just as damaging, stop taking risks. All you will receive from your team members is what they think is safe to say.

When you take responsibility for what goes on in your organization, you model leadership behavior that empowers people. The accountability you want to see at every level must start with you. Your attitude and actions will cascade throughout the organization, creating followership. People will side with you because of what you stand for, even if some of the decisions you make turn out to be less than optimal.

o   Believe it, say it, mean it, and act it. Consistency is paramount.

o   Accept that most communication comes to you because of your title, not because of who you are. Make sure you receive feedback from trusted advisors who will not sugarcoat the truth you need to hear.

o   Don't just change happy to glad. Focus on real momentum changers—those things that make a meaningful difference to your employees, your customers, and your organization as a whole.

o   The difference between good and great is focus. Make sure you always maintain yours.

Leadership Is Rising above "Me" to Embrace "We"

All eyes are always on the leader who sets the tone. You represent something bigger than yourself—you are more than the title; you represent the institution. Your leadership is defined not only by what you do and say, but, equally important, by what you don't do and don't say. Leadership is not a single act or a monumental decision.

Heroism is episodic; leadership is systemic. Leadership is defined by a hundred things, big and small, done every day with consistency and sincerity.

At a recent meeting with our leaders, I did not start by outlining our goals or reviewing charts, timelines, and projections. Instead, I told them the story of a friend, Brent, who had passed away. I had been asked to deliver the closing eulogy. Before I got up to speak at the funeral, however, 33 other people had paid tribute to Brent. Each story built on the previous ones—one moving story after another about how Brent had given so much to others, from financial assistance to a place to stay in his home. Each successive story visibly raised the mood in the church from grief to hope. Brent was not a wealthy man in a material sense, but he was rich in compassion. To me, he was not a "hero" because of a single incident or action; he was a leader because he changed others' lives for the better. The day of his funeral, we could sense our collective moods being lifted even as his body was lowered into the ground. His purpose of making a meaningful difference in the lives of everyone he met will carry on long after his death.

I told this story to illustrate the mission of our organization, Korn/Ferry, which is to enhance the lives of our clients, candidates, and colleagues by delivering unsurpassed leadership and talent solutions. Beyond making money, serving clients, and providing for our employees, our "why" is to change people's lives, much as Brent did. This is the real purpose of our organization. As leaders, we are given the same opportunity to affect others by believing in and pursuing a higher purpose in everything we do.

Leadership is the capacity to translate vision into reality.

—*Warren G. Bennis*

This is the vision that we must convey to our teams, to make them believe that it is possible—especially when the path is uncertain and the way is not clear—and that either we make it together or we don't make it at all.

Leadership is a campaign for the hearts and minds of others, providing hope and being the anchor for courage. It means elevating people above what they had ever thought possible for themselves by giving them a vision and the confidence that they can, indeed, achieve it.

To lead is to inspire, motivating and empowering others.

As a leader, you must move beyond "what must be done" to "why we're doing this." This is the essential difference between a manager and a leader. Without the why, there is no real buy-in; it's just aiming for the targets and hoping for a short-term reward. (Think of it as the difference between renting and owning.) Most important, the why reveals the deeper reasons for the organization's existence.

Leadership is grace, dignity, and restraint. It is how you make other people feel. Your achievement as a leader is measured in their success.

o   Earn trust, but expect loyalty. Respect among team members is nonnegotiable.

o   Words motivate; actions inspire. Model the behaviors that you expect your team to adopt.

o   Never look the other way.

o   Your road is the "high road." Always—no exceptions.

o   Don't get too comfortable. The job—as in *your* job—
    can always be taken away from you.

Summary

A CEO is ultimately in the solutions business, charting the
way. This kind of leadership requires distilling complexity into
simplicity and, in particular, being able to contextualize. During the great recession of 2008–2009, I found myself providing
reassurance, trying to orient the organization to the horizon.
I started by shifting perspective: September 11 was a tragedy.
The economic challenges we faced were merely tough times
that would eventually pass.

For a leader, the only road is the high road. Leadership
is the restraint of power. It is about self-discipline, distinguishing between the urgent and the important so that you can
rise above the immediate. When you're the leader, you can't
just react. As much as you'd like to fire back an e-mail in
response to a diatribe that just hit your inbox or to call someone out for leveling unfair criticism, you cannot be reactive.
There have been times when I have been on the receiving
end of negativity as people chose to vent their frustrations or
voice their complaints. Even when they crossed the line, I
had to choose how, when, and if to respond. As long as there
was no ethics breach, I have found that the best response is
to demonstrate grace.

Grace is rising above and showing dignity so that you can turn problems and challenges into opportunities. Grace is possible only with humility, which reminds you where you came from and that you are speaking for the institution, helping you to shift from "I" to "we." As an individual, you speak from an "I" perspective—your thoughts, your opinions, and even your reactions to what other people say. As a leader, however, you speak from the "we" perspective, with words that echo forever (positively or negatively), especially when they are repeated by others. Never react; instead, ask yourself: is this about *me* or about *we*? If it's the former, forget it and rise above.

CHAPTER 2

PURPOSE

Success demands singleness of purpose.
—*Vince Lombardi*

arge or small, Fortune 500 firm or community group, every organization is established for a reason that goes beyond profit. Far more important is a sense of purpose that permeates every level.

Leadership begins with purpose. It is the "why" of the organization. The companion of purpose is vision. Vision is the "what"—a picture of what the company will look like when your purpose is realized. Together, they form the basis of leadership.

The grander the purpose, the bigger the vision. Purpose fosters alignment across organizations in which thousands, or even tens of thousands, of employees are making countless decisions and taking innumerable actions every day. If these employees have a strong sense of purpose, they are more likely to act in concert with the mission and objectives of the organization. Without purpose, individuals and teams can easily go off track.

As an undergraduate student at Princeton University, William Clay Ford, Jr. never automatically assumed he would join the family business: Ford Motor Company. Upon graduating in 1979, however, he saw that Ford was really struggling as the United States dealt with the effects of the first energy crisis. Being aware of everything that Ford had given him, he felt obligated to help. For the great-grandson of Henry Ford, this was a time to step up to a greater purpose.

Bill Ford has been with the company ever since, moving up through the ranks from his first job as a product planning analyst through domestic and international assignments in manufacturing, sales, marketing, product development, and finance. He became chairman in 1999, and then served as chairman and CEO from 2001 until 2006, when he became executive chairman. Of all the topics discussed in a far-reaching dialogue with Ford—a conversation that encompassed the responsibility that comes from having such a recognizable family name and the renaissance of the Ford brands—purpose elicited the most energy and excitement.

"I take enormous pride in our family name," Ford says. "There are special responsibilities that come with that as well. One thing that the name does is, it certainly makes us different from almost every other company out there. We're not a nameless, faceless corporation. People who know Ford think of it as a family company because they know we're going to be here through thick and thin. And if things go well, that's great; and if they don't go well, they know where to find me, which is different from many companies. At many companies, people can never be sure who is accountable at the top, and who is going to be there through thick and thin. But people know that about Ford. That does place a special set of responsibilities upon me and the company."

> Purpose enables hundred of employees to make thousands of decisions in unison.

Central to the company's vision is Ford's lifelong commitment as an environmentalist. He sees as no contradiction between this and his role as an automotive executive. He has had a strong sense of purpose when it comes to environmentalism for years, and he has been vocal about environmentally friendly vehicles for a long time. "We are fulfilling the vision that I've had since the day I joined the company," Ford says.

Yet people didn't always see eye to eye with him on that purpose — "green" wasn't always the best color for an auto executive. "When I joined the board in 1989, I was told I had to stop associating with any known or suspected environmentalists because I would tarnish my reputation in the company," Ford recalls. "I said, 'I have no intention of doing that.' In fact, I went on to become the first businessperson to address the Greenpeace annual conference in London. That raised a few eyebrows on both sides of the ocean. But I felt we absolutely had to continue down this road and go as fast as we could."

With a name that is synonymous with cars and with the Motor City that was once the capital of the so-called Rust Belt, Ford holds a vision of a greener purpose for himself, his company, and his industry. Today, Ford's vision is coming to fruition with the introduction of the company's first pure-electric vehicle, a revamped product line with cleaner, more fuel-efficient vehicles, and a company that is committed to sustainable business practices. "I'm really excited now that the day is here when the vision is being implemented. My great-grandfather's goal was to make cars affordable. My vision is to make them affordable in every sense of the word—economically, socially, and environmentally," Ford says.

"We pursued environmentally friendly vehicles as fast as we could, but [until recently] the technology wasn't really there. Some may say that I should not have spoken out so early, but to me it was crystal clear. This was exactly the road our industry had to go down. I never wanted to become the kind of place where our employees would have to apologize to their families and friends for working here. If that day came, we would have lost; it would have been an untenable space for us to occupy. So to me, we had to pursue [environmentally friendly vehicles] aggressively."

> *The purpose of life is a life of purpose.*
> —*Robert Byrne*

As Ford's example shows, leaders must immediately establish and live the organization's purpose and vision. In time, with consistency and commitment, the purpose will become a collaborative effort that is grounded in the culture and enhanced with insight from others.

Purpose Is the Soul of the Organization

Purpose extends far beyond making money. Of course companies are in the business of generating profits; to say otherwise is ludicrous. But money alone is not a sustaining motivator for an organization or for an individual contributor. Just as people long for meaning in their lives, so must an organization. Consider a few examples of mission statements that seek to raise the sights of everyone in the organization:

To passionately innovate what is essential to human progress by providing sustainable solutions to our customers.

—Dow Chemical

To make all athletes better through passion, science, and the relentless pursuit of innovation.

—Under Armour

To educate its students and cultivate their capacity for life-long learning, to foster independent and original research, and to bring the benefits of discovery to the world.

—Johns Hopkins University

To connect the world's professionals to make them more productive and successful.

—LinkedIn.com

For the company known for the slogan, "Ford has a better idea," revitalizing the company has meant changing the way the industry was seen: green instead of polluting; one in which efficiency and performance could coexist, instead of being mutually exclusive.

Early on, however, a major impediment to realizing Ford's vision was that in those days, everything was a major trade-off. If you wanted fuel economy, you couldn't have power. Great miles per gallon? You had to have a small vehicle. Even some of the safety features would have had to be compromised.

"Going back a few years, if you had asked the customer, 'Are you an environmentalist?' every one of them would have said yes," Ford explains. "But then if you had started to ask, 'What are you willing to give up for that? Are you willing to give up room?' the reply would have been, 'Well, I really don't want to.' Performance? 'No, I really don't want to.' Pay more for it? 'No, I really don't feel like paying more for it.' The trick for us was to deliver to the customer all the fun, all the safety, all the joys of driving in an environmentally friendly manner, and we can do that now. We are at this great intersection where [we have both] the vision and the technology to deliver the vision."

Through consistency and longevity with the company, Ford has more than proven himself as a leader and steward of the corporate soul. He

Glory lies in the attempt to reach one's goal and not in reaching it.

—Mohandas Gandhi

has spent 32 years at the company since college, and he takes pride in the fact that people know that he is approachable and sincere when he says that he wants honest feedback. But since his family name is on every sign and every product at the company, there were perceptions that he had to address and biases he had to change.

"Because of my last name, when I joined the company I think everybody reacted in a different way," Ford recalls. "Some people held me up on a pedestal; others were determined to show I was only there because of my last name. In the end, neither approach was helpful to me. So I always sought out people who would give me honest feedback, and that was hard to come by as a young person in the company. But I got it, and at various levels. One of the things I take pride in is the fact that I have friends in the company from the executive suite down to the plant floor, where I started working."

> Shared purpose creates a sense of shared urgency.

Meaningful connections and a shared sense of purpose can be developed only over time. For Ford, his deep relationships throughout the company have helped him foster a vision of what the company stands for today—and where it is going tomorrow.

o   Purpose stretches us beyond the imaginable to more than we had ever thought possible. It is the difference between doing well some of the time and doing one's best all of the time.

o   Purpose must be tangible, achievable, and measurable. It is the driving force behind sustainable change.

o   Purpose must be omnipresent—on the walls and in the halls. It must be reflected in everything the organization says and does, from the "town hall" meeting with employees to the annual report to stakeholders—and every e-mail and conversation in between.

o Purpose is inspiration; it is far more than "hitting the numbers" for next month, next quarter, or next year.

Purpose Illuminates the Horizon

Purpose anchors the organization; it speaks not only to what must be done, but to how it will be done. Purpose provides grounding and the ultimate direction for all.

Once upon a time, a faraway kingdom was devastated by drought. The crops failed, and the ground hardened and cracked. And so the king ordered his staff to hire the best digging crew in all the land. The crew arrived with picks and shovels and began digging. Six feet, eight feet, ten feet—the workers kept digging. Finally, they put down their tools. All this digging was absurd! Besides, it was hot, and they had nothing to drink.

Enraged that the crew was refusing to dig any more, the king ordered them put in jail. His wisest advisor, however, asked to speak with the workers. "Come," he said simply, and led the crew on a tour of the kingdom, past the fields that had turned to brown stubble, the children who sat listless in the dust, the cows that were chewing dry straw instead of green grass. "You're not just digging," the advisor explained. "You're bringing life back to this kingdom."

Immediately, the workers rushed back to the task. They dug day and night until they struck water. When the king came to see the well, he asked the crew what had made such a difference in their work. "Once we understood why we were digging," the workers explained, "nothing could stop us until we had finished the job."

The moral of the story: purpose aligns, unifies, and elevates. At every level, people see how what they do contributes to the bigger picture. Purpose is that bigger picture. With purpose, individual members of the team come together, becoming a whole that is, indeed, greater than the sum of the parts. Purpose captures people's hearts and minds.

Purpose needs to be tangible. It does not come about automatically. Slogans won't create it; PowerPoint presentations aren't enough. Everyone at every level of the organization must be able to articulate the purpose, to know why they are working together and what they will accomplish when the vision becomes a reality. As a leader, use purpose to show the team what is possible and what is within reach.

> To forget one's purpose is the commonest form of stupidity.
> —*Friedrich Nietzsche*

"We're a family company and have been for 107 years, but I spend less time worrying about that than I do thinking about where this company is headed and how we can continue to serve society in a way that really transcends just making cars and trucks," Ford says. "To me, that's what really gets me up every morning. I don't worry so much about keeping up a family legacy as such because I think much more about the future than I do about the past."

Purpose enhances engagement—an all-important goal for team development. Shared purpose creates a sense of urgency. A common mindset is established, one with authenticity and commitment.

o   With shared purpose, people pull in the same direction, changing "me" to "we."

o   Purpose must have a long shadow, casting its influence over others, both inside and outside the organization.

o   Purpose is the bridge from "what we've been" to "what we want to be."

Purpose Begins with the Leader, but It Is Never about the Leader

Purpose has nothing to do with you, your ego, or your accomplishments. Whether you are the CEO of a global company or the head of the local PTA, as a leader, you stand for purpose. It is the basis of everything you do. People need to look into your eyes and see the truth of that purpose—what it stands for and where it will take them. If you are genuinely passionate about the purpose, expressing your passion will electrify the entire team. Purpose creates cohesion amid constant, accelerating, and sometimes chaotic change.

At the end of 2005, Ford effectively held the titles of chairman, president, CEO, and COO—all at once. While Ford had a talented team of leaders, none of them had the experience necessary to guide the company through a major downturn, which was what Ford was anticipating. He went to the board and told the members that he needed help—he couldn't do it all himself. When the board asked him what he was looking for, Ford's answer was, "The right person."

"I don't care about the title at all. That's the thing about being part of this company my whole life; I couldn't care less about titles," Ford says. "To me, what was most important was finding someone with major restructuring capability and background."

Ford had to think out of the box and break the usual rules of looking for someone within the auto industry. Finding the right person proved to be a difficult quest until the company recruited Alan Mulally, former executive vice president of Boeing and CEO of Boeing Commercial Airplanes. "Alan has been a fantastic leader," Ford says. "He and I see the company the same way, and we see the future the same way."

> Purpose is the difference between doing well some of the time and doing one's best all of the time.

Ford and Mulally also share common ground when it comes to authentic leadership. For Ford, being true to one's self and one's values is the biggest lesson to be learned about leadership that inspires, enabling purpose to kindle a lasting spark in others.

"The biggest thing about leadership is people have to be themselves," Ford says. "Everybody has strengths and weaknesses. You've got to be true to yourself. You can't say you want to pattern yourself after someone else. Everyone has his or her own unique style. The minute you deviate from that, you're perceived as a phony. So it's important to figure out what your strengths are and what your weaknesses are, and augment those weaknesses as best you can with people who have strengths in those areas. To me, leadership is being honest with yourself."

Ford offers the example of football, which is a sport he knows well (he is the vice chairman of the Detroit Lions). Think of the kinds of coaches who have been successful, he observes. They are all over the map. You've got the tough guys like Vince Lombardi or Bill Belichick; you've got the cerebral types like Tom Landry, Don Shula, and Tony Dungy; you've got the fiery guys like Rex Ryan and Mike Ditka. There is no one blueprint. What they all have in common is that they were all true to themselves. Whatever strengths they had, they accentuated.

"I think it's the same with business leadership," Ford says. "I've seen very effective quiet leaders, very effective motivational leaders, and very effective process-oriented people. It's important that people know what they are going to get with you."

True happiness . . . is not attained through self-gratification, but through fidelity to a worthy purpose.
—Helen Keller

Although leadership styles may differ, purpose is always the motivation and inspiration, the driving force behind the vision. The vision is the destination—the goal and the prize of what you want to achieve.

"The company that innovates wins, so innovation is something that I spend a lot of my time on because that's the future of this company," Ford says. "We want to be the Apple of the automotive world. We're headed there. We have all kinds of cool technologies including vehicles running around with just about any fuel that you can possibly think of, including those with hydrogen fuel cells, compressed natural gas and lots of different biofuel mixes."

To be a leader is to be passionate about purpose—authentically and genuinely. Leaders make purpose their North Star and continually lead the organization toward it.

o Embody purpose. People will watch you and follow your lead. If they know that you believe, they will allow themselves to be convinced.

o Personally shape and continually deliver the message about purpose. You can't say it enough.

o Walk the talk of purpose in everything you do. If you don't, purpose is just the slogan du jour.

o Be grounded in purpose over time, continuing to examine it and intentionally adapting it as the world changes.

Connect the Dots between Purpose and Strategy

Policies, programs, strategies, rewards—everything must be aligned with purpose. People need to understand and believe that every job and every task is linked to purpose. No job is too big or too small *not* to be aligned with purpose. In order to be truly motivated and highly effective, your team needs to see the alignment between what you envision, the values you live, and the strategy you outline to get there.

One additional area in which Ford has shown leadership is in fostering an economic revival in Detroit.

"It starts with manufacturing," Ford says. "We have a very good trained workforce here. We have a university system here that is set up to support manufacturing. But we should be the clean-tech locus of activity here in Detroit and here in the Midwest—the suppliers who will be supplying us as we embark on this clean journey as an auto company ought to be right here."

This change is already occurring. A nontraditional supply base is forming for clean technology, and also for on-board entertainment. "I think there is great opportunity, particularly for the clean technology companies, to locate here in Michigan. People often say that this area is the Rust Belt and manufacturing is a declining job base. And that has been true in traditional manufacturing. But there is the real need now to reinvent manufacturing and to manufacture different kinds of products now than we have in the past. And that's where the opportunity lies," Ford observes.

> *For every man there is a purpose which he sets up for his life and which he pursues.*
>
> *—Quran*

To move forward toward realization of the purpose and vision takes courage. When purpose is lacking, the telltale signs are obvious: fatigue, mediocrity, fractured teams, and goals that are stated, but without accountability. Even if people do well, they rarely give their best without purpose. Adapting to change is difficult, and initiating it is next to impossible. Without purpose, even the best strategies fail.

The only antidote to this type of malaise is real meaning—the "why" of what people are doing. With purpose, it becomes possible to navigate the "what" of the job at hand, and to carry out the leader's intent.

o   Purpose is the difference between something being done and done well, mediocre and meteoric.

o   Purpose is grounded and enduring. Yet how we understand purpose must change as the world evolves.

o   Purpose is the motivation to carry out the strategy.

o   Goals and measures for achieving purpose must be achievable. Successful completion should lead to measurable outcomes and rewards.

Summary

Purpose creates change, inspires possibility, and raises the altitude of the organization. Purpose must be seen and felt every day. It is the beacon that points the organization toward the horizon, the long-term vision. Purpose is the constant through all the upsets and setbacks—and through the unexpected gains and tactical victories.

> Purpose must have a long shadow, extending its influence over others.

Among the unexpected gains and tactical victories that Ford realized during the financial crisis and the economic downturn was the reservoir of goodwill that the company received after refusing to take federal bailout money. "That was not something I anticipated—in fact, I spent a lot of time worrying about the opposite, which would have been people thinking that they had their taxpayer money into our competitors so maybe they should buy those products because they already were an 'owner' of those companies. I felt that was a danger—that they would turn away from us rather than turn toward us. But I've gotten thousands of letters from the man on the street saying things like, 'I'm a small business owner. No one would ever bail me out. You guys did it the right way. I'd like to consider Ford as my next car.'"

With authenticity and vision, purpose, and a plan for the future, Ford is moving his company forward on a road of its own choosing. He stands as an example for other leaders, for whom purpose must be the raison d'être of their leadership.

Dream it. Live it. Be passionate about it. Inspired by purpose, others will become more and achieve more as they give more of themselves. And your leadership journey—anchored in common purpose—will be accelerated.

CHAPTER 3

STRATEGY

*I like the dreams of the future better
than the history of the past.*
                          —*Thomas Jefferson*

To be strategic is to look over the horizon and set a course based on assumptions. When married with purpose and vision (the "why" and the "what"), strategy becomes the "how" and the "when." It is rooted in the leader's thinking about what matters most. Purpose and vision evolve slowly (if they evolve at all). Strategy nimbly adapts to changing conditions without losing sight of the ultimate goals.

Sally Blount, dean of Northwestern University's Kellogg School of Management, is a strategic big thinker. Animated and personable, with the intellect of a scholar, Blount reveals her passion and intensity for organizational thinking as she uses her hands to illustrate a point visually and reaches into an arsenal of broad experiences to provide examples. For her, strategy is far more than the "how-to" of achieving a particular goal, especially a short-term one. Strategy must be closely tied to purpose in order to be meaningful; otherwise, as Blount observes, what is the point of expending all that energy?

"I'm a trained social scientist," she says. "What interests me are the cognitive traits of a leader when it comes to setting strategy. The leader needs to step back from the minutiae and see the bigger picture, to take this lens that is focused on what is right in front of you and move it up to 35,000 feet so you can see the broader landscape. At 35,000 feet, you can pull forward in time to see the future and its opportunities and not just focus on the current moment."

Moving away from the formulaic business strategy approach, Blount zeroes in on the human elements: how a leader must think and act, the importance of cohesion and coherence, and communication at every juncture to foster alignment. A longer-term view and an emphasis on enduring strategy have the potential to do far more than allow an organization to hit the quarterly targets, whether they are earnings for a for-profit organization or rankings for an institution such as Kellogg.

"A good strategy transforms a compelling vision into concrete outcomes—it's all about excellence in planning and execution," Blount says. "There are two challenges; one is finding a plan that makes sense, and the other is execution, taking it from a concept to actually making it happen. Within academics, you have to be very attentive to the process, both in the formulation of the strategy and in the execution. In a for-profit setting, people cede a certain amount of authority and autonomy to the person who is in the top job. In academics, it's different. You have to build trust and use that trust to remind the faculty

> *Sound strategy starts with having the right goal.*
> —*Michael Porter*

why you have this job. You need to show them that you hold the right values and that you are not going to take away their academic freedom."

For the leader, a strategy will not be successful without buy-in, which means gathering input and gaining the trust of everyone on the team.

Strategy Must Fit the Organization

Strategy tends to be an overused word. Too often, senior executives are praised for being "real strategic thinkers" or "very strategic." Well, they'd better be! Strategy is a given for any organization. The distinguishing factor, however, is how the strategy fits the organization.

> Never underestimate the potential for uncertainty, fear, mistrust, and ambiguity to derail a strategy.

"I have never seen myself as the creator of the strategy," Blount says. "I see myself as the identifier and the articulator, because the strategy has to come out of elements other than the self. There are places I personally might like to take Kellogg that I just can't take it, given its culture, its history, and its brand."

To be a strategic leader is to let go of your preferences. As the leader, you have to keep your ego in check—to be focused on the organization and not yourself. It's not about your preferences. It's about being willing to let go of what you personally want. Your job is to get the answer right—not to be right.

"My father was a theoretical physicist at Bell Labs. He did not reward me for being short-term clever in the next 10 seconds; he rewarded me for doing the homework to find the right answer," Blount says. "I have always valued that he pushed me: 'Don't be so quick to reach a conclusion. Listen to what your sister is saying. There may be something there.' He would credit me for finding the right answer, not for being the clever one. My dad gave me a deep appreciation that you have to believe in the pursuit."

For a leader, the obvious piece of strategy is laying out a road map—how to get "there" from "here"—just as any guide must point out the trail. But strategy isn't just about the destination. It isn't linear, as many people think.

"What wakes you up as a leader is asking yourself, 'Does the organization have what it takes to do this? Is there something that I am missing?'" Blount says. "You have to be sure that you have a team around you with its ear to the ground—to make sure that things are going as they should. That's how I protect myself: I listen to my instincts constantly, and I don't assume I am still right, just because I was right before. You have to be open to new learning as time goes on and conditions change in executing strategy. Also, as some people leave the organization and others join that may speed you up or slow you down."

All men can see these tactics whereby I conquer, but what none can see is the strategy out of which victory is evolved.

—Sun Tzu

As strategy is formulated and the direction is set, the leader provides guidance, like the lines on the highway, and then lets the team set off to execute that strategy. A flexible and adaptable strategy enhances the culture of a learning organization that heeds the lessons of the past to realize the dreams of tomorrow.

o   When you encounter a new idea, societal trend, or business model—anything that is new and interesting—ask yourself what it means for the future of your organization. How will it affect the execution of your plan, if at all?

o   Communicate continually with all parts of the organization all along the journey to the desired destination.

o   Own the strategy and empower others to implement it. Never underestimate the potential for uncertainty, fear, mistrust, and ambiguity to derail a strategy.

Strategy Is the How

Leadership is having aspirations for what the organization can become and forging the road that it must travel to reach that goal. Strategy is dynamic—and it is far less about planning in the calm than it is about decision making and course correcting in the midst of the storm. Strategic thinking must be perpetual. Woe to the strategist with only one idea.

Creating a strategy requires a high-level plan for applying energy and resources over the long term. It is all-encompassing: it takes into account customer needs, organizational capabilities (current and future), competitive challenges and differentiation, and creating value for stakeholders.

Since taking over as dean at Kellogg in July 2010, Blount

has led the organization through several notable initiatives. The first is "rearticulating what Kellogg is," which includes an advertising campaign with the tagline "Think Bravely." The campaign gives a nod to Kellogg's legacy, Blount notes, while underscoring the belief that business can be "bravely led, passionately collaborative, and world changing."

Another area of focus has been developing a new strategic direction for Kellogg aimed at the 2020 global marketplace and outlining a five-year strategic plan for moving from concept to action. That process addressed four objectives: leveraging and strengthening Kellogg's culture and brand; building and anchoring its global architecture, including its global alumni network; identifying intellectual themes to serve as a foundation for its competitive positioning; and redefining its product portfolio and curricula to align with its key themes. This endeavor may require hiring new faculty and supporting research in new areas, knowing that not all research projects may pan out. "But the ones that do will be intellectually and socially important and will form the foundation of our reputation going forward," she notes.

> *A good plan is like a road map: it shows the final destination and usually the best way to get there.*
> *—H. Stanley Judd*

Blount has also put in place a strong senior team to restructure how the school operates. The goal is to create an organizational structure that fosters operational excellence in student experience, faculty research and teaching, alumni engagement, corporate partnerships, and marketing and communication.

Beyond the tactical choices focused on achieving specific goals, strategy encompasses shared perception. Although the leader sets the strategy, it is not a solo effort. The more the leader listens, the stronger the strategy becomes, with greater buy-in and a sense of shared destiny, which in itself is strategic. In order to embrace the plan, people need to understand not only the big picture of the strategy, but, more important, how they contribute to carrying it out.

o   Acknowledge that strategy does not belong to the leader alone — it is a shared plan for achieving a shared vision.

o   Focus on the "how," not the "how-to."

o   Remember that 90 percent of strategy is execution. Sweat the small stuff and anticipate the big stuff.

Strategy Is the When

Strategy is a road map, purposeful and definitive. Yet it is also flexible and adaptable, responding to an ever-changing environment. Strategy starts with the results of today and lays out the path to the future. It is more than just the road to travel; strategy is also the time needed to reach the destination. Speed is the leader's prerogative, but it cannot be dictated in a vacuum. Set the tone for growth and change, but always move at a pace that your organization's structure and culture can absorb. Tap the brakes before economic curves and accelerate through the turns.

Strategic thinking, like many leadership attributes, is developed over time through experience and exposure to new ideas. A recognized expert in negotiation and behavioral decision making, Blount has been associated with prestigious institutions: the University of Chicago's Booth School of Business and New York University's Stern School of Business, as well as Princeton University, her undergraduate alma mater. She began her career in the Chicago office of Boston Consulting Group (BCG), where she was among a small group of young professionals who spent time with BCG founder Bruce Henderson in his later years.

"BCG was my first job after college, so I became imprinted by the thinking that Bruce was known for: find your competitive niche and what distinguishes you," Blount says. "Frameworks about strategy can be taught, and they make a huge difference. They organize thought and give people language."

> Strategy is far less about planning in the calm than it is about decision-making and course-correcting in the midst of the storm.

More recently, Blount credits the influence of colleagues who mirrored the nuances of strategic leadership, such as making sure that the leader moves at the right speed for the organization. "I partnered with a terrific associate dean of students in my last job as dean of the undergraduate college at NYU's Stern School of Business. She'd let me know when I was pushing the pace with people," Blount says. "She'd say, 'Sally, you've got to let up a little bit.'"

You cannot move the organization at a pace that is faster than people can handle and the organization can absorb. Just as you can't go 20 miles an hour in the fast lane or 100 miles an hour in the slow lane, appropriate velocity is everything for an organization. Strategy (as we'll discuss in Chapter 9, "Navigate") isn't confined to an annual exercise; it needs to be part of the day-to-day thinking and decision making. So, yes, strategic thinking is important, but that's just for openers. The finesse of strategic leadership is in the pace and velocity, matched with culture and readiness.

"You have to take a really hard look in the mirror," Blount says. "Am I stretching the organization farther than it can go, conceptually or temporally? I make sure there are five or so key people I keep in touch with. When something is on my mind, I ask them if my intuition or my concern is grounded or not based on what they are hearing in the organization."

> *Without strategy, execution is aimless. Without execution, strategy is useless.*
> —*Morris Chang*

Strategy requires continuity and consistency. At the same time, strategy needs reality checks. Measure where you are at all times—how much ground you have covered and the distance that remains to the next destination.

"You should create metrics," Blount says, "but it also gets back to communication, communication, communication. Top managers have to get together. Face-to-face interaction still makes a difference. You have to do it with some frequency because you have to replace the old mental schemas of who we were with new ones of who we are. There is no other way to make those changes but with time and communication."

As you plan for where the organization is going, make sure that the team is capable of taking it there. Develop and acquire strategic competencies at the individual and organizational levels to realize a shared vision of success.

o   Differentiate between the important and the urgent. Devote yourself to the important and delegate the urgent.

o   Be resolute—give strategy time to work, but don't be stubborn. If some piece isn't working, be open to modifying it.

o   Establish the length of the runway—the timeline for executing the strategy. Be challenging, but realistic. Don't push the organization farther or faster than it can go.

Strategy Is Execution

Strategy is making a bet—a calculated bet, that is. No matter how visionary the strategy may be, it must also be tactical and practical. It is better to have a strategy that is 75 percent perfect, but 100 percent executable, than a strategy that is 100 percent perfect, but only 75 percent executable. Results are what matter most. Execution requires clarity about what must happen at the intersection of how and when. Continually question the strategy. Gut checks are essential. Is it really working—are plans truly executable—or is change required?

"The thing that hampers strategic thinking is to assume that the future will look like the past," Blount says. "How the game was played in the twentieth century is not the way you are going to win in the twenty-first century. So strategy is that ability to move the lens through which you see the world really far up to scan the full horizon—on both a content level and a temporal level with a forward, future focus—because we have to go somewhere new, not somewhere we have already been."

Consider the fable of the Armstrong Widget Company, a fine, family-owned establishment now run by the great-grandson of the founder. Although the Ace Widget product line had expanded over the years and was solidly profitable, certain practices remained in the dark ages. As the newest executive in the family to run the company, John Armstrong committed himself to modernizing the company. He brought in consultants to help him analyze the company's process-es and systems and determine where improvements could be made. Task forces were formed, and managers and employees were engaged in every level and department.

> *Ideas are easy. It's the execution of ideas that really separates the sheep from the goats.*
> —*Sue Grafton*

Whenever inefficiencies and convoluted processes were identified, the consultants would drill down to find an expla-nation. The answer was usually "that's the way we've always done things" or "that's how we do things around here." Mak-ing changes was a slow uphill battle at times.

During one of the regular status meetings, the consul-tants presented a particularly challenging problem in one of the company's oldest product lines. What should have been a three-day production process was stretched out to four as the finishing stage that could have been done late in the third day was not started until the fourth. As the consultants and the company engineers began to consider how things might be improved, John Armstrong asked his 90-year-old grandfather if he remembered the rationale behind the production process.

"Ah, yes," his grandfather replied. "Chester, the manufacturing manager, never wanted to run the production line too late in the day because he liked to go fishing. We never missed a shipment, so I never saw the harm in it."

"When did Chester leave the company, Granddad?" John asked.

"Let me see—about 1971."

As this story shows, strategic thinking requires simultaneous attention to the here and now and to the future—where the organization wants to be in three years, five years, or longer. Strategy honors the past, but is not hampered by it. It bridges the gap between preserving the brand and the heritage and moving boldly in new directions.

o Establish and uphold the values and culture of the team. Everyone should know what the organization stands for and where it is headed.

o Be continuously curious and willing to find the new how. Be inquisitive, but don't conduct an inquisition. Always have a Plan B—and a Plan C.

o Don't just talk about values; embody them. They are at the heart of your strategy.

Strategy Is Culture

Strategy requires tough decisions: what the organization will and will not do in order to preserve its brand, honor its history, and realize a future that is of its own making. Short-term pressures to achieve certain results and benchmarks are relentless. Have courage in the face of these quarterly and even monthly challenges. Never lose sight of the forest, and the trees will take care of themselves.

> Strategy starts with the results of today.

When you spend so much time developing the process and setting strategy, it gives you insight into how you have to implement that strategy. You need to know who your blockers are, and which people are going to be your enablers and implementers. Your goal is to energize and empower those people, and really make them understand how the piece you are handing them will tie into the greater whole. The life of the senior leader is all about communication.

"I spend all day listening to others and then describing to them what I see," Blount says. "It's so fascinating amid all our advances in science and technology: The limiting factor in our ability to build strong organizations is just humans' ability to all get on the same page and go in the same direction."

You can't ignore someone who is a blocker and is resistant. How much political heft—how much squawking power—does this person have? Is she likely to make a lot of noise? Whenever possible, through communication, engage those people in the process.

"There are three general reasons why people block—substance, respect, and pace," Blount says. "First, if people have a problem with the substance of the plan, it is because they believe you have it wrong. So you need to sit and listen to them because they could be right. They are closer to the elements than you are. You may not have the content of the answer right. The second reason people often block is because they are the long-timers who have been there—certainly longer than you. You need to honor their

Endurance is nobler than strength, and patience than beauty.

—John Ruskin

experience with listening and respect. Because if they don't feel heard, they will block you, and here again you often learn something. The third reason people block has to do with timing—not the change itself, but the pace. When people feel rushed, that leads to rigidity. They may agree with the answer on a concept level, but they will get rigid if you push the pace too fast. This is how you determine if you need to adjust your timetable."

Nothing replaces taking the time to walk the halls and engage with the blockers one-on-one. They are blocking because they want to be heard. "And you can't always be the one—there's just not enough time in a day. You also need deputies walking the halls," Blount says. "You need a team when [you're] setting strategy and implementing it."

And as with everything else that defines a leader, setting and implementing strategy requires that a leader do more listening than talking, giving others assurance, and always leading the way with the confidence that comes from having a team that shares a commitment to excellence in execution.

o   Don't try to go it alone—you will fail. Effective strategy depends upon others.

o   Establish a culture of learning. Elevate the ability to do something new and different on the individual and organizational levels.

o   Be the chief culture officer, the enforcer and defender of what the organization stands for. Be the lens that sees mistakes as learning opportunities, not failures.

Summary

Strategy, rooted in values and purpose, gives encouragement through times of ambiguity and uncertainty. Strategy without purpose and values is a short-term plan that is directed toward shallow goals.

> Focus on the how, not the how to.

"I have to believe in what I am doing," Blount says. "If I have that, I can execute just about anything. I have to believe in the product and where we are going. Life is too short not to. I want to help make the world a better place. I decided at midlife that if we, in academics, don't stand up for those values, who will? I believe education makes a difference, and that's what drives me. That is what gives me boldness in setting strategy and executing it."

Strategy sees the possibilities, but does not ignore the realities. It drives effectiveness, accountability, and performance. Strategy is tangible and tactical, always seeking to promote growth and enhance competitive advantage. Moving from roadblocks to buy-in, strategy that is embraced broadly creates followership. By addressing the short term while always focusing on the long term, strategy answers the questions how and when as the organization executes against the plan. Strategy charts the course forward from what is believed today to what is dreamed tomorrow.

CHAPTER 4

PEOPLE

He who gets the best players
usually wins.

—*Bobby Bowden*

Despite all the technological innovations of the past century, a simple truth remains: talented people make businesses successful and organizations great. Over time, your results will be only as good as the people on your team. But rather than simply being a collection of stars, your team must become a mosaic of talents and abilities that work together, complement one another, and carry the organization forward.

Assembling that mosaic—attracting, aligning, developing, and stimulating the team—is the very essence of leadership. However, it doesn't just happen. Motivated, talented, and ambitious people have many opportunities open to them. To attract and retain talent, leaders of successful organizations rely on the power of engagement. Those who are truly engaged in what they do and the organization for which they work are not easily lured away to pursue other opportunities.

One company that thrives on the talent of its team is Cirque du Soleil. From its humble beginnings on the streets of Quebec City in 1984, this privately held, Montreal-based entertainment company has grown into a spectacle of remarkable circus arts and entertainment, earning such descriptions as "incredible" and "awe-inspiring." Today, Cirque du Soleil has 5,000 employees, including more than 1,300 performers from 50 countries. Over the course of its history, it has entertained more than 100 million people in 300 cities on six continents. With high standards and a commitment never to disappoint an audience, Cirque du Soleil continuously raises the bar on the expectations for its performances.

"My biggest kick in life is to catch people by surprise," says Daniel Lamarre, CEO of Cirque du Soleil.

> When you're the leader, it's never about you, but it starts with you.

Recruited by the founder, Guy Laliberté, Lamarre joined the company in 2001 and became CEO in 2006. For him, having the right people (including those who can walk a tightrope, defy gravity on a trapeze, juggle, bend into complex contortions, and so on) is crucial.

"We are all very inspired by the performances of our artists because, at the end of the day, they are the ones who make a difference for all of us," Lamarre says. "They have no choice but to perform at a very high level because, in their jobs, they have thousands of people watching them. If they don't do something perfectly, someone in the audience will notice. My ultimate goal is that other people, even if they are all by themselves in an office, will think and act as if there were people watching what they are doing."

One of the defining leadership attributes is establishing and maintaining a connection with people. In the case of Cirque du Soleil, that means attracting the best talent—and attracting millions of customers each year. "As I have said many times, in 'show business,' the show comes first, because if you have a great show, you have a great business," Lamarre says. "If you don't have a good show, you don't have a business. We have a saying here when we open a new show: let the show do the talking. If the show is good, then people will come. The expectations for us are getting higher and higher, and that's the pressure we feel every day."

Without the talent, there is no show. But talent alone is not enough. Talent must be married with vision to create an effect that leaves the audience spellbound and enthralled, and begging for more. Then marketing, promotion, logistics, and numerous other departments must ensure that show does, indeed, go on.

Ultimately, the success of a company can be measured by how it develops its team, with a deep bench of talent that can grow and rise through the ranks. Creating opportunities, encouraging those who aspire to learn and do more, and utilizing the talents of more experienced people as mentors can make a real difference.

"There are a lot of young people in this organization who have their own dreams and want to succeed—the average age at Cirque is 30 years old," Lamarre says. "That adds a lot of dynamism to the organization. The older people working here—and some of them have been here since the founding of this organization—are used as guides. The leader needs to make sure there is a good blend, having guides who make sure that the young people don't reinvent the wheel, while letting the young people remain enthusiastic. We are also very conscious of the importance of training people and making sure they can grow within the organization. For example, there are former artists who have become coaches and then artistic directors. That says a lot to someone who is 30 years old, who can see one of his or her colleagues has grown within the organization. That is the best message you can send."

> The leader sees how the pieces fit together, a mosaic of talents and abilities that create a team that is powerfully diverse in its perspective, ideas, abilities, and experience.

As research has shown, what creates engagement and generates happiness is the ability to experience progress on a daily basis. And, let's face it: your people have got to want to work with you, the leader. How you treat and empower others will be the deciding factor. People rarely leave careers; usually they leave jobs and bosses. But, once again, it's not about you; it's always about the team. Just as an extraordinary teacher is most interested in how much the students learn, as a leader, you need to concentrate first on developing your team.

"In our meetings, we make sure everybody has an opportunity to communicate his or her point of view," Lamarre says. "It doesn't matter from whom the idea comes. If you are invited to a meeting, it is because you have something to say. You are expected to participate, not just attend. I'm also probably the only CEO who has a clown working for him. I hired this person a few years back to make sure that I never forget the business I'm in. So we have this character who makes sure that we are not taking ourselves too seriously. Madame Zazou is there to inject a sense of fun—and a little madness—into the workplace. As a natural free spirit and mischief-maker, she is unpredictable and uses cheerfulness, playfulness, and surprise to ruffle some feathers among the established order."

As human beings, we are wired to evolve personally, to become more tomorrow than we thought possible today. At Korn/Ferry, I maintain two perspectives as the leader of the organization. One is "outside-in," to understand how our clients perceive and interact with the firm, along with top-line sales, innovation, and new products. The other view is "inside-out," to understand what employees experience. Do they feel cared for? Are they treated fairly? Do they know that what they do matters? Are they given opportunities to be stimulated and developed? As a leader, my job is to inspire and motivate every person on my team to stretch and grow, becoming more than even she thought possible.

> *There are three things extremely hard: steel, a diamond, and to know one's self.*
>
> *—Benjamin Franklin*

Leading Others Means First Leading Yourself

When you're the leader, it's never about you, but it starts with you—the behaviors and attitudes that you model, the example that you set. Your personal accountability becomes the measure of everyone else on the team. In order to lead others, you must continually monitor yourself—not overestimating your strengths, and not underestimating your weaknesses. Let others illuminate your blind spots as you improve yourself and, by extension, the organization. Understand the tremendous responsibility that goes with the privilege of the corner office; that where much is given, much is also expected.

When a leader's ego and ambition go unchecked, his ability is severely undermined, and this can result in organizational defeat. In 1815, having recaptured the French throne, Napoleon Bonaparte engaged in a bloody battle against his enemies in the small Belgian town of Waterloo. Facing the Duke of Wellington, who commanded British and allied troops, Napoleon was confident of a quick and easy victory. Yet when a frontal attack failed to rebuff the British forces, Napoleon's army was driven into chaos and confusion by an intense counterattack. In the end, 25,000 of Napoleon's troops were dead or wounded, and 8,000 others were taken prisoner. Napoleon was forced to abdicate the French throne a second time and was ordered into exile until death on the remote island of St. Helena.

This above all: to thine own self be true.

—William Shakespeare

Consumed by his own ego and his ambition, Napoleon failed to recognize the strength of his adversary, the Duke of Wellington. As a result, he "met his Waterloo." For any leader, overestimating her own abilities and underestimating the competition are a fatal combination.

Trust in leaders starts with credibility and competence, and it is heightened by genuine caring for others. Leaders build two-way trust through communication and transparency, with feedback and coaching provided along the way. Hold yourself accountable for what you say you will do, and expect the same from others. Live the values of the organization in your walk and talk.

o   Never confuse what you do with who you are. Leadership begins with who you are as a person.

o   Look humbly in the mirror. Self-awareness and honesty go hand in hand. The more you can see yourself, the more honest you become.

o   Instill a "say/do" ratio of one to one—do what you say, and say what you mean.

o   Demand accountability from others, but as the leader, you must accept responsibility.

To Win, You Must Have the Right Players

It all comes down to the talent, competence, and readiness of the members of your team. Pick people to fit the strategy—those who are strong where you are weak. Seek a variety of backgrounds, skills, experiences, and approaches. You do not want a team of yous. Rather, you want a team that works together.

"We are truly international—we have employees from 49 different nationalities," Lamarre says. "If you walked into the cafeteria in our studio in Montreal, you would feel as if you were at the United Nations. It doesn't matter if someone is Canadian, American, Russian, or another nationality. We look for someone who has a global perspective, because we spend a fair amount of time traveling around the world and meeting with people who come from different backgrounds and cultures. If you work with Cirque de Soleil, you can work here for many years, and you can grow with our organization. If you want to have an international career, this is a good place. If you love show business, you will have a great time."

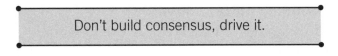

Don't build consensus, drive it.

One potential drawback, however, is that an artist who is in Tokyo one day and Taipei the next might lose the perspective of the head office: why the decision was made to do this or do that. That's where leadership can bridge the gap in perception and understanding, by reaching out to the team so that everyone understands the plan and how to execute it. For Lamarre, that means visiting the Cirque shows in each of the countries in which it operates.

"When I visit them, I explain what happened last year at Cirque and what our plans are for next year," he says. "I spend hours answering every single question they might have. Also, if there is a problem on a touring show, I bet you that my vice president will fix it before I get there!"

Open dialogue between the leader and the team fosters a culture of openness and inclusion, especially in the area of diversity of thought and ideas. "What is important is that the best idea prevails," Lamarre says. "I have worked in the corporate world where there was a lot of politics, and sometimes politics will overtake a lot of good ideas. Here, we don't mind people debating as long as the best idea wins."

In some organizations, one person has a lot of power, and the herd tends to follow that person's recommendations. Someone who is new to the organization doesn't have the power base to step forward with comfort and credibility. When the leader is willing to listen and respond, people feel empowered to ask questions and make suggestions.

No coach has ever won a game by what he knows; it's what his players know that counts.

—Paul Bryant

"I will personally answer questions from any of our 5,000 employees," Lamarre says. "They know they can raise questions, and they can e-mail me [with] more questions at any time of the day. I stay close to the action. I always come back with new ideas and new suggestions. I spend a lot of time listening. By listening to employees, I have been able to change things, not just for their benefit, but for the good of the organization."

The lesson for leaders is to challenge traditional views and perspectives and encourage unconventional thinking. Diverse viewpoints can offer a new look at old problems. But don't hire people simply for what they know; hire them for who they are.

o   Choose hunger and drive over pedigree and capability.

o   Know that people are both creatures of habit and instruments of change. Help your team strike the right balance between these elements.

o   Ingredients alone are not enough; they need blending. Relentlessly drive alignment within the team while embracing diversity in all forms. Push for accord rather than consensus.

To Lead Is to Coach

As a leader, your job is to coach—to be a guide; to be a teacher; to be a motivator. You need to connect with all your constituencies, translating your vision for different audiences. The buttons for each person are different. Adapt and adjust your message to make sure your audience is listening—hearing *and* feeling the message.

As a leader, you need to help others to see the horizon, so that your vision becomes their vision. Your players cannot win if the information they need is in your head and not in theirs. Remember, it's the players who win the games, and it's the coaches who lose them.

I grew up playing competitive sports, so when I was in my twenties, it was a fairly easy transition for me to begin volunteering as a coach of youth basketball teams. My style then was neither very sophisticated nor very mature: it was all about winning. Now, as the father of five children and a coach of both boys' and girls' basketball teams, I approach coaching very differently. My goal is to teach each player to be a leader. At the start of the season, I don't talk about winning the championship. Rather, I explain that the purpose of this season is to teach each of the players what it takes to be a leader, and not just the "stars"—all of them. As I tell the players, "We're all in this together. We're only going to be as good as the least experienced person on the team. We're going to win or lose as a team."

This past season, our team won the championship, but that was not the highlight of my time coaching the team. The most important moment for me was our very last practice. One of the boys on the team had not played a lot of basketball, and he had started the season unsure of himself. Over time, he had grown in confidence and skill, but he still clearly saw himself as not being as good as the other boys. On that last practice, I ended the routine the way I always did: The players would have to run sprints unless someone on the team could sink a three-point shot. When I asked who wanted to take the shot that would spare the team from the dreaded sprints, all hands went up—except that of the one boy. I handed him the ball.

> Self-awareness and honesty go hand in hand.

As he walked to the three-point arc, I could see the doubt and questioning in his eyes. He took the shot, and the ball hit the rim. Then I did something I had never done before: I gave the ball right back to him. "Shoot again," I told him.

This time the ball went through the net. The whole team erupted in cheers for the player. When I saw the expression on his face, I knew that this was the highlight of the whole season for him, just as it was for me. Later, his father confided in me that sinking that basket had meant everything to his son. That was the real victory of the season, more than winning the championship. Each player, especially this one boy, had learned the importance of believing in himself and in one another.

A coach's job is to develop the person, not just the player. Each individual's development is far more important than the numbers on the scoreboard. That is shown by the example of coaches like John McKissick, whom I profiled in my first book. As the coach of the Summerville, South Carolina, Green Wave, McKissick has amassed a record as the "winningest" coach in football: 576 victories in 58 seasons and counting. Yet his focus is always on the individual, caring more for the person than for the outcome of any particular game. Or Bob Hurley Sr., the longtime coach of St. Anthony's, a poor parochial high school in Jersey City, New Jersey. A demanding, old-school basketball coach, Hurley has racked up more than 1,000 victories, as well as 23 state championships, 10 Tournament of Champions titles, and three national titles. (In comparison, when the legendary John Wooden concluded his 40 years as head coach at UCLA, he had won 885 games.) More than his numbers, Hurley's passion as a coach is to develop the character and discipline of the young men on his team, many of whom come from underprivileged backgrounds.

> To understand the nature of the people one must be a prince, and to understand the nature of the prince, one must be of the people.
> —Niccolò Machiavelli

Be a leader who acts like a coach, creating an enthusiastic environment in which everyone wants to engage. You don't want drones; you want people who are creative and empowered, who think and look for opportunities, and who generate breakthrough ideas. Celebrate creativity and risk taking. Establish a culture of teamwork and trust. Make people believe in themselves, in the team, and in the organization.

Just like great coaches, true leaders are not just interested in winning. They know that the proverbial journey is far more important than reaching the destination. It's not the prize, whether it's a trophy or the next quarter's numbers. It's getting there through the efforts of the entire team.

At Cirque du Soleil, Lamarre has taken steps to broaden the concept of the team, particularly when it comes to shows that have yet to be unveiled. "In the past, all the executives were entitled to see a show in development. But we thought that was not good enough. We have so many employees who didn't have the occasion to see the evolution of a new show. So today, it doesn't matter if you're in finance or HR or whatever department, our studios are open to any employee," Lamarre explains. "Now, on any given day, employees can just walk into the studio and watch a rehearsal. That is very much appreciated by the employees, who now feel as if they are part of a big secret, which is the new show we are creating. That's fantastic for creating the sentiment of belonging to a culture."

o   Provide energy; don't consume it. It's up to the leader to empower the team.

o   Show your team members that they are part of something bigger than themselves.

o   No matter what the conversation—even if you are firing someone—everyone who comes into your office should leave feeling better than when he walked in.

Leaders Are Known by the Company They Keep

The effectiveness of your team is determined by its weakest members. You have to give people the time and resources they need if they are to develop their skills and competencies, but you should also know when to admit that it's not working. If someone cannot be successful in her job, it's time for her to leave. There should be no equivocation about it. The fit factor is everything.

"If you are looking for a job [where you work] from eight to five and then you go home and be quiet, it won't be here at Cirque du Soleil," Lamarre says. "We have to sell tickets every day, and there is always something happening on the site of a show. So every day you have to change your agenda. The logistics aspect of what we do is crazy because we tour with a huge infrastructure. You can take any time of the day—two o'clock in the afternoon or two o'clock in the morning—no matter what time of day it is, there is at least one or two shows in presentation somewhere in the world. You can receive a call at any time because something is happening in Japan or Australia or Moscow."

> *Success comes from knowing that you did your best to become the best you are capable of becoming.*
> —*John Wooden*

Ultimately, though, the leader is accountable for the results of the team. If the results aren't there, you are responsible. If your team does not perform up to expectations, you must find out why and make the necessary changes. As the leader, you must focus on what truly matters, and make sure your team understands the priorities.

As Lamarre observes, "If I talk to a business manager, the first question is not, 'How many tickets did you sell?' It's, 'How is the show?' We have a department called 'quality of show.' We have a show in Las Vegas that has been running for 18 years. We need to make sure that the performance is at the level that it should be—the costumes, lighting, choreography. The person who bought a ticket tonight deserves as good a show as the person who saw it 18 years ago."

When a player is in the wrong position, make the change right away. Do not prolong the inevitable. If you have given consistent feedback, the change will not come as a surprise to the player. If it does, then you have failed as a leader.

o "One more chance" is often one too many. Making a change quickly is best for all involved.

o When you conquer conflict, teams coalesce. Help people leave their past habits and learn new competencies.

o Show graciousness, even if you are showing someone the door.

Summary

Leaders are facilitators on the sidelines, but they are never removed from the front line. The leader can't be the star player, scoring all the points. Rather, the leader must be committed to helping others to do their best. Set high expectations for your team members, and help them to see what they can achieve.

Belief is in the leader's eyes and on the leader's lips. Everything you say and do must affirm the vision of what is possible.

"We sell emotion and passion and laughter, and being scared about what an acrobat can do," Lamarre says. "That's what's driving us. We always try to catch people by surprise. One of the comments that I hear often is, 'You did it again! I've seen five or ten of your shows, and every time you surprise me with something new and innovative, romantic and poetic.' That's part of who we are."

The leader sees how the pieces fit together, a mosaic of talents and abilities that create a team that is powerfully diverse in its perspective, ideas, abilities, and experience. Help your team to develop in a way that exceeds what individual contributors could accomplish on their own. Instill pride—in people, in the team, and in the organization to which they belong.

CHAPTER 5

MEASURE

However beautiful the strategy, you
should occasionally look at the results
—Winston Churchill

A ll companies do the expected: they measure the top and bottom lines, margins, costs, and so forth. Most of them also have metrics for the operating environment, the competitive landscape, and customers. But how many of them actually do something with the data?

Effective leadership requires data and the hard, indisputable facts, but that's only the beginning. Results are never an endpoint. More important than the results is what you do with them. Act and react. Design and redesign. The purpose of measuring and monitoring is to carry you forward into action. Moreover, even in this era of the "virtual and viral," "eyeballs and Web ecosystems," nothing replaces your own eyes and your

Don't tell people how to do things, tell them what to do and let them surprise you with their results.
—George S. Patton

touch. Direct feedback from your team, your employees, and your customers will help you to identify where the organization is successful and where it is missing the mark. Then it is up to you to interpret, redesign, and act. In the end, it's results that matter most. Performance is the ultimate equalizer.

Measure and Monitor Your Own Progress as a Leader

As my Korn/Ferry colleagues have found, leadership demands self-awareness and an insatiable appetite to learn. Other things being equal, self-awareness is the trait that rises above the rest. Leaders who are self-aware balance self-confidence and humility. Self-aware leaders are realistic not only about their own strengths and weaknesses, but also about the organization's.

Kevin Plank, CEO of athletic performance apparel, footwear, and accessories manufacturer Under Armour, starts and ends his day at the whiteboard in his office. On that board are the four objectives against which he measures his ability to drive the company forward: making great products, telling a great story, providing great service to clients, and building a great team. Each day, he maps out what he needs to do and what he has done to further each of those goals.

For Plank, a former University of Maryland football player, this type of self-assessment goes back to his days on the gridiron, when improvement in performance could be tied to a few distinct, but important factors, from diet to drills. He knew that by making even minor changes in those performance metrics, he could drive himself toward greater achievement. Today, he applies that mentality at his company, emphasizing what he knows will make a difference, such as making sure that he listens more than he talks and making "big bets with big partners" as the company aligns itself with top collegiate teams and professional athletes.

For Plank, the internal metrics of his company are only the beginning. He and his team know that what matters most is the performance of their customers: the athletes who wear their products. If Under Armour apparel can help shave a tenth of a second off a sprinter's time, or if it can lower the body temperature of a football player by half a degree so that a starter can stay in the game longer, then it has made a measurable difference where it really counts.

> More important than the results are what you do with them.

"Whether you are sweating or pouring water over your head to cool off, you know there is nothing worse than a soaking wet cotton T-shirt, which can weigh $2\frac{1}{2}$ to 3 pounds," Plank says. Inspired by his days as a college athlete, when "nobody was thinking about what athletes were wearing under their uniforms," Plank used his own personal measure of discomfort to envision a different kind of T-shirt, one made from stretchy, snug-fitting fabric that calls to mind women's lingerie. After getting samples made and passing out the shirts to friends and fellow athletes, Plank knew he was onto something.

"If you had asked me back in 1996 what the company would look like in the future, I wouldn't have been able to tell you when we would cross the $1 billion in revenues mark or when we would have 5,000 employees," says Plank. "I wouldn't have told you exactly how I envisioned it. Instead, I got up every day and said, 'Why not us?'"

To answer that question, Plank has relied on the discipline of measuring: always knowing where the company and its products are now, where they can expand, and what can be improved.

"One of the first rules I learned was from a great American company, Milliken and Company, which is a leading textile and chemical manufacturer," Plank says. "On one of my trips to Milliken and Company in Spartanburg, South Carolina, as I learned more about fabrics and construction, one of the things [I was told] was, 'If you aren't measuring, you're just practicing.' Today, I'm a big believer that measurement is paramount. If I were to sum it up, measurement is the heart and soul of what we do."

> Let others judge the results; you discover
> the implications of the results.

Just as vision needs execution to become reality, so execution needs relevant and meaningful measurements to ensure that what is being done will actually get the organization (and its customers) to where it wants and needs to go. Operating without the benefit of relevant measurement and feedback is like driving in new territory without a map. Yes, you will be in motion, but you won't know whether you're really getting anywhere.

But don't limit measurement to the organization. As the leader, you must be cognizant of how your decisions, actions, attitudes, and behaviors are moving your team forward—or keeping it back. The world will bypass the static leader. You become enlightened by soliciting feedback from everyone around you. This can be an informal daily routine. For example, when I am traveling or when I haven't seen a colleague for an extended period of time, I usually ask, "What should I or the organization be doing more of or less of?" Whether you use a formal process such as 360-degree assessments or engage others informally to obtain feedback, you need to know how you are perceived. None of us can see ourselves clearly or objectively. Only by being willing to subject yourself to the mirror of honest feedback can you measure where you've made progress and where you have room to improve.

Measuring your performance as a leader requires transparency and candor that can be uncomfortable. You have to put yourself under the microscope for others to view. If you do not take this step, however, you will have only your own opinion and partial feedback from those around you (who may tell you only what you want to hear) to guide your actions. Good never became great with limited input.

As part of a recent leadership meeting at Korn/Ferry, I invited our team to do a real-time review of me. Using "clickers" to ensure anonymity and our predefined leadership characteristics that are linked to our strategy, my direct reports rated my strengths, blind spots, and weaknesses in front of me. Suffice it to say, it was a grueling two-hour session.

> *Truth will ultimately prevail where there is pains to bring it to light.*
>
> —*George Washington*

My motivation for conducting this real-time review of myself was to move the team from observational to operational leadership, working as a team. The best way to do that, I decided, was to set the example. As I began the session, I held up a mirror and told them, "It starts with you and me." Then I announced the rules of engagement for the assessment. They were shocked! For me it was a risk, asking people to rate me based on what they thought of me as a leader and as a person. The feedback I received, however, was incredible. Equally as important was the impact that it had on the team.

At the end of the session, I went around the room and personally thanked each person for participating. I handed each of them a small mirror as a reminder of this exercise and the need for all of us to take a good, hard look at how we are perceived. This type of feedback is an invaluable measurement of how the leader is perceived and how well she can inspire others to follow. As I experienced, only by being open and accepting of feedback could I actually learn how others perceive me.

- o Formally and informally, ask for and accept feedback from others.
- o Whether you are winning or losing, learn from the results.
- o Let others judge the results; you discern the implications of the results.

Lead by Walking Around

No matter how much a dancer practices at the ballet barre, what counts most is her performance with others. So, too, it is with leadership. Leaders seek feedback on what can be improved, make the change, and measure the outcome. The process is continuous; the leader is always seeking ways of doing things better in order to achieve the desired results. Such improvement does not come from casual engagement, but from a deep commitment to monitoring and measuring.

"Leadership is making people want to follow you," Plank says. "We are very team-oriented. Don't get me wrong; we are hierarchical. At the end of the day, it's my decision—the CEO's decision. That type of authority is important, but the number one rule is to empower your team. In a company of 5,000 people, I probably have 15 people I call 'engines.' They are the ones who drive the company. They create energy, and people want to be around them. They make things happen. As the CEO, I want to get the day-to-day responsibilities off my plate and let others run with them. Give people the tools they need to be successful."

At Under Armour, getting things done requires the effort of the entire team. For Plank, the success of those efforts is gauged by specific performance measures, from sales figures to new product development. Specific measures will vary from organization to organization, yet what is common to all is the need for the leader to gather feedback broadly and from every department and at every level.

Although I review some key performance indicators on a daily basis and others weekly, as the CEO of Korn/Ferry, I have found that the best indicator is talking to and observing our customers and employees (the "outside-in" and "inside-out" perspectives, as described in Chapter 4). Through the tone, cadence, and content of the feedback I receive, I can glean what no computer screen, website, e-mail, or spreadsheet will ever reveal. I can gauge the subtleties of whether the organization is engaged and aligned to the purpose, vision, and strategy, as well as where the opportunities and challenges can be found.

Whenever I travel to another country or city, I make a point of visiting our offices and employees. I always get the purest and best advice and input from our clients and from employees who are on the front line, which is the intersection of strategy and execution. Several years ago, when we were in the early stages of transforming our mono-line brand, focused on executive recruiting, to multiple lines of business by moving carefully outside of our core offering, I visited one of our large operations. As one of my colleagues gave me a tour, introducing me to all of the employees, I noticed that she skipped three individuals who were sitting in interior offices. When I asked who they were, she replied, "Oh, you don't need to meet them. They are with our new business," as if they were not part of our company at all.

Do what you can, with what you have, where you are.

—*Theodore Roosevelt*

I bit my tongue and kept my reaction to myself. However, I made a point of welcoming these newcomers to the company. That night, as I flew home, I was so upset by how these employees had been dismissed that I crafted a "One Company" strategy, which today is the basis for how we operate. Had I not taken the time to visit the office and walk around to meet everyone, I never would have seen what was happening, including what needed to change to create unity and alignment.

o   Leadership is not found behind a desk. It's found among the people.

o   Talk to the constituencies that matter most—your employees and your customers.

o   Seeing is believing; listening is understanding.

o   Listen more than you talk. Act on what you hear.

Keep Your Finger on the Pulse

Just as a pilot continually watches the instrument panel, so must you. Establish a dashboard with metrics that register whether you're on course to reach your goals and realize your vision.

With the drive and single-minded focus of an athlete, Plank measures by the numbers—and not just revenues and earnings. Under Armour's marketing and promotion strategy has always centered on selling products to athletes and teams on the high school, collegiate, and professional levels. The company is the official outfitter of numerous collegiate athletic teams, and also sells products internationally to European soccer and rugby teams. There is also a long list of sponsorships agreements with individual athletes.

Plank measures the business by team sponsorships and agreements to outfit athletes and by the launch of direct-to-consumer marketing. In a very real sense, the number of athletes, the number of teams, the number of sports, and the number of products—all these very real and tangible numbers—add up to how successful Under Armour is in executing against its strategy.

"Our products are seen on the field, which gives them exposure to individual consumers, including through the Internet, television, magazines, and live at games," Plank says. "This exposure helps us to establish authenticity and credibility with consumers, who see our products being worn by high-performance athletes. The fact that these players are wearing our products shows that they're in our community."

> Avoid becoming the leader of the inevitable,
> who allows the future simply
> to determine itself.

The only reason those athletes are wearing Under Armour apparel, Plank knows, is because of the performance improvement that it provides: speed, strength, endurance, and results. If the products fail to deliver, athletes will soon have a different shirt on their backs. In order to keep outfitting athletes, performance apparel must live up to its promise of heightened expectations.

"The best merchants are those who dictate what's cool, not the ones who predict it," Plank says, "and then they build that credibility with consumers. Steve Jobs told us, 'iPads are cool and iPhones are really cool.' Howard Schultz [founder of Starbucks] told us that coffee is cool. Same thing for us, I hope. We are building credibility with consumers. Great brands are meant to have a point of view."

Credibility is reinforced by measurement, making sure that the message that is delivered is the message that is received. Otherwise, it is very easy for perceptions to become reality. Consider a humorous story I recently heard. In late fall, a group of settlers in the remote village of Outpost were preparing for winter. The group's leader, who had never been taught the old ways of reading nature's signs around him, could only make a guess: the winter was going to be cold, and the people should gather firewood. Then one day, he traveled to the nearest town and called the National Weather Service, which confirmed his suspicion: the winter was indeed going to be cold. The leader ordered more firewood to be collected. A week later, he checked in again with the National Weather Service. It had amended its forecast—it would be not only a cold winter, but a very cold winter. So the people of Outpost gathered even more wood.

> *Don't measure yourself by what you have accomplished, but by what you should have accomplished with your ability.*
>
> —John Wooden

When the leader checked in with the National Weather Service a third time, the prediction was now for a very, very cold winter. Finally, having asked for every branch and twig to be gathered, the leader asked the National Weather Service how it could be so sure. The answer: "The people of Outpost are gathering an awful lot of firewood."

Don't be caught up in what become self-fulfilling prophecies. Rely on measures that are real and data that are meaningful. Let heroic aspirations guide your way forward, but never lose sight of the here and now. Today's results place you at a tangible mile marker. Measure the distance between where you are and where you want to be.

o   Choose metrics that measure the path to success without straying into the trivial.
o   Establish targets and timelines along the journey.
o   Don't question, ask questions.
o   Continually recalibrate the downside.

It's Not Just the Results—It's What They Say

Measurement helps you avoid becoming the leader of the inevitable, who allows the future simply to determine itself. Rather, you must learn not only from the past, but also from today in terms of your results in real time to ensure that you are consciously shaping tomorrow.

Measuring the obvious is obvious. When my kids were very young, I was always amused when I went to their sporting events. No score was kept—at least, not officially. Yet, whenever someone asked someone else how Sally or Bobby had done, the immediate response from parents was whether the team had won or lost and by how many points. Even when you are not keeping score, people keep score. For a leader, it's not the score; it's what the score means. With meaningful data, continual improvement is possible.

"I want Under Armour to be the hub of technology—to have the world's greatest vetting system," Plank says. "We are, first and foremost, all things technological—fiber, fabric, and function."

If you are measuring, you will most assuredly discover what does not work—the ideas that looked promising, but that turned out to be failures. However, trying and failing is never a mistake. The only real mistake is not being willing to make mistakes. They can be the purest form of improvement, provided you learn from them. In the pharmaceutical industry, for example, drug failures often lead to new discoveries, such as different and more effective uses for compounds from what had originally been theorized. In order to gain the knowledge of those results, however, you have to pay attention to what they're saying.

"In business, decisions are never black or white, yes or no, right or wrong," Plank says. "They are typically gray, and it's the responsibility of the leadership to make them right or wrong. If they end up being wrong, you have to put your ego aside and admit, 'I made a mistake.' When people become more protective to avoid mistakes instead of driving for results, that can be very dangerous. Under Armour is a very aggressive company. We drive. We indicate the tempo. We walk with a purpose. That keeps us entrepreneurial."

> *Obstacles are those frightful things you see when you take your eyes off your goal.*
> —Henry Ford

One of those CEO decisions that became a turning point for the company took place in late 1999, when Plank decided to spend $25,000 on a magazine ad. This was a risky move, since the company didn't have extra cash lying around for an ad campaign that might or might not work. But he decided to go for it.

"At the time, we had $5 million in annual sales," Plank says. "We were lucky enough to have a product placement in the movie *Any Given Sunday*—an Oliver Stone picture with an all-star cast. We had sent product to the production office. Oliver Stone had never seen our brand before, and he said it would be perfect for the movie. That was unbelievable exposure! Now we needed to see how we could capitalize on it. We talked about running our first national ad in *ESPN* magazine. I can still remember: we had 15 or 20 people. We had these roundtables where we'd ask everybody for their input. The ad was going to cost $25,000. The response was, 'We need inventory . . . we need fabric . . . we need equipment . . . we need people.' We ended up running the ad, and it generated $750,000 in revenues. Without that, I don't know if we would have made it through the spring of 2000."

This is not just the stuff of spreadsheets and bar charts; it's about measuring what's *not* on the reports and spreadsheets— what you can find between the lines only when you synthesize the data and connect the dots that others cannot see.

- It's not just the "why" and the "what" of your results—it's also the "where to from here."
- Performance is not absolute; it is always relative. Never lose sight of the competition.
- Strategy is executing and adjusting continually. Use results to guide you in real time.
- If you focus only on today's goals, tomorrow will come before you're ready for it.

Summary

Measuring, monitoring, and metrics matter. Don't suffer from the "Mirror, mirror on the wall" syndrome, relying on what you believe to be true: that you have the most inspiring purpose, brilliant strategy, and talented team. Measure and monitor so you know whether that's true.

On an Excel spreadsheet, everything works. Even if it appears that you have the right strategy and processes, they must be validated. Doing so means going beyond the metrics. Walk around. Talk to people. Listen. Look into their eyes and see for yourself whether the strategy is really working.

> If you focus only on today's goals, tomorrow will come before you're ready for it.

Never confuse measurements with data. The facts and figures are where the process begins. The true value-added is in knowing what those results mean. Is the organization living up to its purpose? Is the company delivering value to its clients and customers? What about innovation, reaching new consumers, and widening the competitive edge? Without measuring, it is impossible to answer these questions. But the answers alone are not enough. From answers must come action: for the leader who seeks continual personal improvement, and for the organization that drives steadily forward toward success.

CHAPTER 6

EMPOWER

As we look ahead . . . leaders will be
those who empower others.

—*Bill Gates*

The bridge from planning to action is empowerment—of others, not yourself. Empowerment, however, is not something that you can give or do to someone else. It cannot be dispensed like some magic pill or miracle serum. People must empower themselves. As the leader, your job is to inspire them to do so.

Few people understand this as well as Peter Guber does. During more than 40 years in the entertainment business, he personally has been the producer or executive producer of numerous blockbuster movies that have earned more than $3 billion worldwide—box office hits such as *The Color Purple*, *Midnight Express*, *Batman*, and *Flashdance*. His films have garnered more than 50 Academy Award nominations; one of these was *Rain Man*, which won Best Picture. In 2011, Mandalay Entertainment, of which Guber is the chairman and CEO, made the film *The Kids Are All Right*, which won the

Golden Globe's Best Motion Picture Award and was nominated for four Academy Awards, including Best Picture.

"The best managers and the best businesspeople are those who can narrate their offerings to their customers or audience," Guber says. "You have to make sure the audience is listening. If you can't do that, people will not buy in."

In addition to his entertainment career, Guber is a full professor at the UCLA School of Theater, Film and Television, and has been a member of the faculty there for more than 30 years. He stresses to his students that narrative power is the key to establishing an emotional connection with the audience—whether that audience is employees, customers, or anyone else the leader is addressing.

"When a leader can find a way to emotionalize his message, then people feel that he is talking to *them*—his audience, his customers, his clients, his patrons, his colleagues," Guber says. "If they can own the message emotionally, they can play it forward. They grasp the narrative. Then, when they tell it to others, they are telling *their* own story."

Like the shaman of old, who was the keeper of the stories and who passed on the wisdom and the lore of the tribe, the leader is the master of the organization's narrative. Drawing upon many sources—history, sports, personal experience—a leader spins tales of how others exceeded expectations, beat the odds, and accomplished the seemingly impossible. Story is far more than the recitation of facts and data points; it is pure inspiration and aspiration. When they listen to the story, people become caught up in the emotion. They ask themselves: if others could do this, why not us? Why not me?

"Leadership is storytelling in a way that becomes memorable and actionable," Guber says. "Storytelling is as old as human beings. About 40,000 years ago, if we [hadn't] worked together and used language, we wouldn't have survived. So you could say leadership is a 40,000-year-old process. We were able to climb to the top of the food chain because of social language and interaction. Story enabled our ancestors to remember the facts that were told in an emotional way. It's the same with a company or with a product. We are social creatures. That's how we are made. That's what LinkedIn and Facebook and Twitter do, too. They make us social. "

> The leader is the master of the organization's narrative.

There are communal experiences that really bring home this point. One was the 2011 British royal wedding between Prince William and Kate Middleton. It was estimated that two billion people—one-third of the world's population—viewed the royal wedding. Another compelling event, by coincidence, happened just a couple of days later: the capture and killing of Osama bin Laden by U.S. Special Forces. For many in the American public and elsewhere, this was a rallying cry for freedom. These two separate and very different events showed the power of emotion as part of the story.

What made those two events memorable is not just what people saw, but how they felt. This is the connection that happens when you have an event that catalyzes everyone. Emotion is aliveness, the feeling of being here, now, and fully present.

For the leader, the challenge is finding ways to tap into that emotion to forge a connection. It starts with the leader. How can people follow you if they don't feel that they can trust you?

"When a leader walks into the room, before he or she speaks the first word, people already have an opinion," Guber says. "That's the way we're wired. Language is an art to express ideas, but energy is what is projected. So when you go into that room, you need to be on your game. Own [the] ideas that you are expressing so that others will embrace what you are saying."

From the earliest humans to today's leaders, people have used their innate ability to tell stories to connect with others. A story that touches people's hearts packs an emotional punch that enables them to grasp what is possible—for themselves and for the organization. That is the essence of empowerment.

Not Power—*Em*power

Empowerment takes root when a leader is willing to delegate opportunities, not tasks. As a leader, you cannot make all the calls. You must delegate the authority for decision making, too. A goal of leadership is not to tell people what to do, but rather to tell them what to think about. Enable and equip others, and then get out of their way. You can't just say, "People are our most valuable resource." Show it. Let people feel your sincerity and honest caring, that you know their goals and plans. Make *their* career development *your* priority. Help others to grasp their own heroic aspirations. Believe in what they can achieve. When the passion comes from the leader, people will be more likely to empower themselves.

"The leader can support people in changing their trajectory," Guber says. "If that can happen early on, a person's whole career—his or her whole life—can be changed for the better. For the leader, that means coaching and mentoring and assisting and supporting. People have to find that they have what it takes inside. A highly effective way of doing that is by using story, including [stories] from the leader's own life. Use the tools that are available to you. But here is one tool you cannot use: you can't tell them, 'This is what you are doing. Here [are] the manual and the instructions.' They can't do it your way. They can't 'do' you—like an actor in a role. They can't do your act, because then they will fail. They have to do it their way."

> When people feel empowered to do more,
> they will become more.

When you become a leader, you know that you can accomplish your goals only through others. There is no room in the orchestra for a one-man band. Leadership is not about the use of power, but about the leader's restraint in using power. True leaders do not worry about undermining their authority when others become empowered. They care most about enabling others and making the team successful.

When was the first time you felt empowered (and, no, getting out of diapers doesn't qualify)? For me, it wasn't far from the bottom of Maslow's hierarchy. Right after the basic needs of food, clothing, and shelter were tying my own shoes and learning to ride a bicycle. I can still remember marveling at others as they tied their shoes. I was absolutely mesmerized with bewilderment and hoped that these long, thin laces could magically form a union. Make a loop, wrap the other lace around, pull another loop through . . . I tried over and over again. When I finally achieved this audacious goal, I was truly amazed—liberated and empowered by what I could do myself, for myself.

After conquering shoelaces, the next big milestone was riding a two-wheeled bicycle. Some 44 years later, I can still vividly remember my dad removing the training wheels from my shiny Schwinn. The day was cold and cloudy, but when my father put his hand firmly on my back and gave me one hopeful and final push, it was as if the sun were shining warmly on my face. I pedaled down the street as if I owned the road.

From tying your own shoelaces to providing shoes for others. From your parents caring for you to caring for your parents.

> Surround yourself with the best people you can find, delegate authority, and don't interfere as long as the policy you've decided upon is being carried out.
> —Ronald Reagan

From memorization of data to comprehension of facts to application of knowledge. These are the natural cadences in life as we mature. What we never forget, however, are those first moments of accomplishment, when we felt freedom, joy, and pride in what we were able to master. These are the same feelings a leader must evoke in others through empowerment.

"A leader can use metaphors, examples, analogies, and events from history to help people see the picture," Guber says.

"Maybe it's the leader's own struggle, or maybe it's something another employee struggled with. The story shows that someone else was in a similar position and was able to do something about it. Now others see that the ability they need is within their grasp. They can do it by leaning forward, by putting out the right energy, and by throwing caution to the winds. They will be able to transform [their] experience and, by extension, the product of their experience. The truth is, they may not win. People will not always be successful in everything they try. But the journey brings so much more joy, and people will learn so much through the process, that the next time, they will win. The trick is, it's *their* journey."

For a leader, the evolution is always from one to many as others are empowered. Inspiring the team members means rekindling in them the joy of learning a new task, of mastering a new skill, and catapulting them forward with self-sustaining energy and belief in what they can and will accomplish.

The team's engagement is directly proportionate to the leader's inspiration. The leader willingly steps aside, speaking last during brainstorming sessions and listening attentively to contrary opinions. Leaders do not want to be surrounded by "yes people" who agree with everything they say simply because they said it. Leaders want empowered people who can access all of themselves—their thoughts, ideas, experiences, beliefs, and values. The more empowered people become, the stronger the team.

o   When people feel empowered to do more, they will become more.

- ○ A team of "yes people" isn't a team, it's a dictatorship.
- ○ Don't confuse differences of opinion with disloyalty. Empowered people should speak their minds.

Delegate Responsibility, Not Accountability

Delegate for development. People grow when they are stretched, but you are accountable for making sure that they are not stretched too thin. Just as with strategy (the "how"), your job is to communicate the "what," the "why," and the "when"; leave the "how-to" in the hands of your team.

One of the finest examples of success achieved through delegating responsibility is the story of Commander D. Michael Abrashoff, who set a new standard for Navy ships with his transformation of the USS *Benfold*. Among the phenomenal results that Abrashoff produced was leading the *Benfold* to win the prestigious Spokane Trophy for having the best combat readiness within the Pacific Fleet. It marked the first time in more than a decade that a ship of its class had received such an honor. And the *Benfold* would never have been so recognized had Abrashoff not empowered his crew.

The crew's proficiencies and abilities, and the ship as a whole, were to be rated on 24 areas, on a scale ranging from basic Level One, which was the required minimum and was usually considered good enough, to advanced Level Four, which, until Abrashoff and the *Benfold* came along, there appeared to be no incentive to reach.[1] Once he recognized the tremendous potential of his crew, Abrashoff abandoned his goal of reaching an overall rating of Level Two and raised the bar to Level Three, much to the chagrin of many of the Pacific Fleet's other commanders. When he was initially faced with the challenge of not having enough senior people to supervise the 24 areas of testing, the commander ordered his combat systems officer to pick supervisors from the next group down. Abrashoff reasoned that he didn't necessarily need a senior person in charge; instead, he could empower a young, third-class petty officer to whom he could delegate. Abrashoff assigned senior people to the most demanding areas, and then put more junior people in charge of other responsibilities. The lower-ranking officers were so honored to be chosen that they worked hard enough for several of their teams to outshine those supervised by senior people.

By breaking out of stratified systems and empowering more people, Abrashoff essentially unleashed people with talent and let them rise to levels that no one had expected. He did it simply by challenging them to make the *Benfold* the

> *The beauty of empowering others is that your own power is not diminished in the process.*
>
> —*Barbara Coloroso*

readiest ship afloat. Four months later, the Navy's top boss, the chief of naval operations, streamlined the assessment process and ultimately settled on a formal program that allowed ships to skip the six-month training process if they could achieve the same performance levels that the *Benfold* had achieved. This model became the standard throughout the Navy, and it came about because Abrashoff and his officers delegated responsibility to people who turned out to be ready and able to accept it.

Empowerment is all about raising people's sights concerning what they can do and what they expect of themselves.

"Empowerment as leadership is not me giving something to you," Peter Guber says. "It's helping you find the resources so that you can empower yourself. It's not me saying, 'You can do it.' It's each individual finding the way. The leader acknowledges the challenges facing them and recognizes that they are up to it. But people need to metabolize their ability to be better than they thought they could be."

The organization simply will not scale if you micromanage. As the leader, you must scale yourself through others, extending your reach and magnifying what can be accomplished through the efforts of others. Give direction, but don't try to do it all. Set the boundaries, and then get out of the way.

o   One multiplied by itself is always one. You need an empowered team to reach the critical mass that will make a difference.

o   Check in and stay connected, but don't check on. Leadership is not the "gotcha" business.

o   You own the mistakes; empower the team to own the victories.

o   Understanding of the mission is imperative. Voicing differing perspectives in private is helpful; agreement with the strategy in public is nonnegotiable.

Inspiration Is in the Stories You Tell

Given my background as a finance guy, when I was promoted to CEO, I wondered whether I could be "inspirational" enough. I quickly realized that inspiration wasn't something that you get from a book or a five-step program. It is not a unilateral action. It requires making connections with others around some of the most basic human emotions. Inspiration requires authenticity, and it is best done through storytelling.

> You own the mistakes; empower the team to own the victories.

"People need to look into your eyes and see that you are authentic," Guber says. "If they perceive you as authentic, then people will run—feet, heart, and tongue—all in the same direction. When you are an authentic leader, people will listen to you in a completely different way. They really get what you are talking about, because your intentions speak loudly and broadly. If you are not authentic, that will shine through, too."

Storytelling reminds us of who we are, what we believe, what we value, and what matters most. We love the stories in which good defeats evil, the hero saves the day, and love conquers all. And we all cheer for the underdog because we can identify with the one who was never expected to win, but who—through sheer determination, some skill, and an awful lot of luck—gets the prize.

I was in a movie theater recently, watching a film in which the underdog hero rose up against seemingly insurmountable odds to become victorious. At the end of the film, people actually clapped as the credits were being played. Why? Because they connected emotionally with the story. Or, think of the movie Rocky, a fictional rags-to-riches tale of an unknown boxer who suddenly gets a shot at the world heavyweight championship. Even though Rocky loses the fight in a split decision by the judges after 15 punishing rounds, he is the champion for whom the audience always cheers. (The movie went on to win three Oscars, including Best Picture.) Even today, the

Nothing can stop the man with the right mental attitude from achieving his goal; nothing on earth can help the man with the wrong mental attitude.

—Thomas Jefferson

iconic image of Rocky running up the steps of the Philadelphia Museum of Art and pumping his fists in the air evokes the heart-pumping determination of a character who could not be empowered until he believed in himself.

Stories inspire us and move us to consider what we might become if we, too, were "more"—more determined, more prepared, more confident, and more empowered. As a leader, what is the story you tell? Do you show endless PowerPoint slides with pie charts and bar graphs? Or do you tell a story that really matters, infused with emotion that uplifts and inspires people?

"In the beginning of the movie *Superman*, there is a scene in which he is beaten up by a bully," Guber says. "It's 20 seconds long and doesn't have much to do with the rest of the movie. Then the whole movie is played out, and Superman says at the end that there is one more thing he has to do. The audience always cheers. They know what he is going to do: he is going back to take care of that bully. People don't like inequity, you know. They just don't like it. And that's the other thing. You could watch the movie in Slovenia with subtitles, and it would be the same thing. People see things the same way."

Acknowledge the challenges, but always illuminate the way forward with the light of hope and unshakable confidence. Wear your heart on your sleeve, if necessary, to paint a picture of what you truly believe can and will become the reality.

o   PowerPoints never touched anyone's heart; pie charts can't evoke emotions.

o   Eloquence can never overcome a lack of authenticity.

o   Project confidence; build courage; imagine possibilities; give hope.

Make Others' Needs Your Personal Calling

Inspiration developed through a common purpose and a vision provides self-sustaining motivation. Your purpose—your own personal calling—must be to make others feel important, to let them know that they truly matter *to you*. Let others see that you are part of the team, that you are one of them. The greater your accessibility, the more you inspire others.

"People need to see that you are all in the same boat," Guber says. "They want to know the leader has some skin in the game. If they think you are not interested, then you're not interesting to them—and they won't listen to you. But if you are interested and interesting, they will open their hearts to you. This is what leadership means: to help people own the process and do it well. It's the job of the leader to inspire people to have a positive attitude and to put it on steroids. Attitude drives their aptitude! Inspiration moves the whole thing forward when you energize their attitude."

I experienced the power of accessibility firsthand as I walked through the streets of a small Mexican town with former president Vicente Fox. It didn't matter that he had been the leader of a sovereign nation; that day he was a private citizen—the owner of a nearby ranch and hacienda where his family had lived for decades. Strolling along cobbled streets, Fox's accessibility was disarming. There were no handlers; nothing about his presence drew attention to him.

At one point, he excused himself and hurriedly crossed the street. At first, I could not see where he was going, then I saw him stoop his tall frame and wrap his arm protectively around the shoulders of an elderly woman who had been walking slowly down the other side of the street. As I watched, he listened attentively and then spoke privately to her. She turned around and headed in the other direction, leaving me to conclude that she had been lost or confused. Had it not been for this helpful man, whom she probably did not recognize as being the former president of her country, the woman could have kept wandering.

> *The mind is everything. What you think, you become.*
>
> *—Buddha*

When he rejoined us, Fox picked up our conversation where he had left off. He did not mention the woman. His actions, however, spoke volumes about his character as a leader—that he truly does care for the people with whom he closely identifies.

Over the months since that visit, I have thought back on that scene, recalling not only what I saw, but what I felt. I was in the presence of a great man. Everyone mattered equally to him. With genuine caring, he had taken it upon himself to ensure that everyone found her way.

By their words and actions, verbally and nonverbally, leaders need to touch and inspire others. For Guber, one inspirational leader was a coaching assistant from his college days. "I learned a lot from sports in college and playing different sports," he recalls. "We had a really great coaching assistant who was the leader, but wanted to show he was really part of the team. So he didn't occupy the seat at the head of the table. You can't put on a badge and make people like you."

Effective leaders convey the feeling that they are with you, that what you do matters, that it's important. That is an empowering feeling.

o   Give of yourself: your time, talent, experience, and wisdom.

o   Never be too busy for someone. A great leader is most concerned with the least of all.

o   Do your good works in private, never calling attention to yourself. Otherwise people will question your sincerity.

Summary

Empowerment means enabling and equipping others to make decisions. It means delegating authority so that hundreds of people can make thousands of decisions that are directionally in line with your vision. When leaders inspire people to empower themselves, to stretch and grow, and to be creative and innovative, failure is inevitable at times. Be behind your people in success and in front of them in defeat. You have to recognize that failure is inevitable; it's part of the road to success. You can't have a culture in which people are punished for failure instead of a culture that learns the lessons from failures and then turns setbacks into success.

> PowerPoints never touched anyone's heart.

"It's toxic when people fail at something and the punishment is exile or death," Guber says. "The fact is, failure helps people become better because they learn. The question is: was it a thoughtful exercise of intelligence and creativity? The leader needs to disabuse people of the attitude that failure is a bad thing, per se. Let's say that a studio has sixteen movies. They figure that four will be mega-hits, four will be for [home video] distribution, four will be breakeven, and four will be flops. You've got a business in which [some] of the time, the projects fail—and the bigger the project, the bigger the failure. So do you execute somebody because of that, or do you accept the statistical probability? Think about what we teach kids about baseball. When the player is at bat, he can strike out seven times out of ten and become a multimillionaire. It's always a statistical analysis."

As people move through their career development, leaders need to coach them to embrace opportunities to increase their skills and experience. There's more urgency to that approach now than there's ever been, with the average tenure of a CEO of an S&P 500 company today being about five years. If you truly want to empower people, you need to show them that you are interested in their lives and their careers. That's why leadership is coaching and mentoring, and especially assisting and supporting younger employees.

"What happens is, people start at the bottom of the pyramid, and as they work their way toward the top, their view gets narrower," Guber says. "We've been designed to look at things that way. But these are false rules. Things have changed. It's so pervasive. In the C-suite, it's $3^1/_2$ years, 4 years, 5 years, and then out. So how do you cope with that change? How can you inspire and empower others? You have to turn that pyramid over so that you are at the point. Then, as you look ahead, your opportunities continue to widen, not narrow, as you go forward. If you don't do that, the world will become a scary place. To be a leader today is to recognize that you don't know how long you will be in a particular position, nor do you know how long people will be on your team with you. But if you can empower and inspire others, you can get the most out of them for the time that they are there, and make an impact on their futures."

The era of 40 years with one company and a gold watch are over. The same goes for your top team. The paradigm has shifted. You have to do your best in the time you have.

"If you can get five, six, seven years out of your really good employees, that's great," Guber says. "Maybe you only get two or three, and then they move up—great! You are only renting them. As a leader, your attitude has to be, 'I understand that you want to move on.' You [need to] create that environment, in which people know that you understand their career needs, and that in three or four years, they will probably move on to the next better thing."

The leader's job is not to empower people, but rather to help them to empower themselves. It is the difference between ordering people to do something and inspiring them to see what they can do. When they are highly motivated, they will willingly stretch their reach as they become empowered and attract others to the journey. With story and example, help others to raise their sights and their aspirations. Let them imagine all that they might become. Then get of their way and let them surprise you.

CHAPTER 7

REWARD

I've learned that people will forget what you said, people will forget what you did, but people will never forget how you made them feel.

—*Maya Angelou*

 hen you mention the word *reward*, people automatically assume that you mean money. Sure, the paycheck, the bonus, and the all-expense-paid trip are all tangible elements of a reward system. Money, however, is ephemeral—and it certainly cannot buy everlasting loyalty (although it may be able to rent it temporarily). For leaders, it is much more important to sustain the intangibles that can to turn casual followers into fervent believers. How? Reward and celebrate every step of the way.

Reward and celebrate the incremental achievements, not just the final results. This communicates progress, inspires others, and reinforces successful, repeatable behavior. Reward and celebrate the big wins—a new customer, a major contract—that grow the business, as well as the progress. When people feel appreciated, they will do more.

At the heart of the matter, people want to know that they belong, that they are an integral part of something that is bigger than themselves. Even love, which is rarely talked about in discussions of management, is not so far-fetched a concept, because leadership requires followership. Thus, it needs an emotional connection. Why should relationships in business be any different from any other relationship? When the leader communicates, "You are appreciated," "You are important," and "Your contribution makes a difference," what he is really saying to each contributor is, "You are loved." Communicating your respect and appreciation—your love—to the team is transformational. Then your team members will take the mission and purpose to heart, elevating themselves and the organization to the next level.

> To lead means to be in charge of the "care and feeding" of those who follow.

Vineet Nayar, who is CEO of HCL Technologies Limited, believes it is nothing less than revolutionary to recognize that the employee is the core differentiator and value-creator of the company. As he sees it, handing the baton to the employees is perhaps one of the highest forms of acknowledgement of the worth of the team.

When Nayar became CEO of HCL in 2005, the company was rapidly losing its luster. A pioneer in India's emerging information technology (IT) services sector at its inception in 1976, HCL was among India's top five IT companies. By 2005, however, it had become stagnant, with slowing growth and a declining market share. The company needed a shake-up.

Nayar injected new life with an overhaul of the company's culture, putting employees at the top of the value pyramid, rather than at the bottom. His philosophy "Employees First, Customers Second," was viewed as aberrant in conservative corporate cultures. But Nayar, who had graduated from one of India's top business schools and joined HCL as a young MBA, is a self-proclaimed "believer in the power of transformation." He had long believed that command-and-control, top-down leadership was ineffective and suffocating for employees.

"I have always believed that organizational focus and structures should be inverted to focus on the 'value zone'—the place where frontline employees interact with customers and create real value for them. All rewards, recognitions, and corporate priorities should be focused on this value zone," Nayar says.

His approach worked. In the five years after Nayar took over as CEO in 2005, revenues and operating income more than tripled, the number of HCL customers grew fivefold, attrition among the 58,000-plus employees in 26 countries dropped by 50 percent, and HCL was named "Best Employer" in India and Asia by Hewitt Associates.

Many CEOs claim that their people are the company's most important asset, but how many of them actually walk the talk? By recognizing the strengths and talents of their team members—an important component of reward and celebrate—leaders are able to unleash the potential of others. In turn, when their efforts are recognized, people will stretch themselves to see a brighter future, a bigger tomorrow than the status quo of today.

"When you think about great leaders, heroes like Gandhi and Nelson Mandela, what they did was, they created dissatisfaction with today. There are lots of companies that are not growing, but I don't think they're unhappy with themselves," Nayar says. "So the first thing you need to do is make [a company] unhappy with[itself,]and then you need to create the romance of tomorrow, where you can be free or you can be great or you can be number one. And then you must tie those strategies together."

Taking a leap of faith, Nayar turned his organization upside down, rewarding and empowering employees who create the real value in the company by putting them at the top so that they would no longer be hampered by traditional hierarchies. In this new HCL, the managers became accountable to the people who created the value.

> *Everyone wants to be appreciated, so if you appreciate someone, don't keep it a secret.*
>
> *—Mary Kay Ash*

"The role of leadership is perhaps the most difficult to define in companies that compete in a knowledge economy," Nayar says. "One of the structural flaws of traditional management systems is that the leader holds too much power. That prevents the organization from becoming democratized and the energy of the employees from being released."

With reward and celebrate, the leader steps out of the spotlight and shines it on the team instead. "It's all about you," becomes the leader's message.

Easy to Say, Hard to Do

You can never say "good job," "thank you," and "I believe in you" too often. Simple verbal recognition for a job well done is a powerful motivator. Praise and encouragement are enduring rewards for the soul.

Frederick Winslow Taylor is regarded as the father of scientific management and was one of the first management consultants. He sought to improve industrial efficiency, and his ideas were highly influential during the period of social activism and reform that flourished from the 1890s to the 1920s. Taylor died before the now-famous employee motivation studies were conducted at Western Electric's Hawthorne plant, near Chicago, Illinois, in 1924, the results of which undercut a core pillar of Taylor's belief: that workers were motivated purely by economic gain.

> If it sounds simple, it's not;
> if it seems obvious, it's elusive.

The studies were intended to examine the influence of environmental variables on a group of production workers. The group was divided into two subgroups: a test group, which would undergo environmental changes, and a control group. The members of the control group would work under normal, constant environmental conditions. The researchers began by manipulating the lighting of the test group. When the lighting for the test group was increased, the group's productivity increased—but the productivity of the control group increased as well. This result was somewhat unexpected, since the lighting at the workstations of the control group had not been altered. The researchers concluded that productivity increased because of the attention from the research team, not because of changes to the experimental variable. The experiments at the Hawthorne plant thus showed that people are mainly motivated not by economic factors, but by emotional factors, such as feeling involved and receiving attention.[1]

Leaders today should be that "light" of attention on their employees. If you know that people thrive when someone pays attention, then you must notice them—consistently and genuinely.

Demonstrate to people through your words and actions that you are aware and that you appreciate their efforts. Foster a performance- and achievement-oriented culture by praising not only extraordinary results, but ordinary efforts as well. Otherwise, the pendulum could swing the other way.

"Building strong interpersonal relationships based on trust is perhaps the first step in this direction," says Nayar.

"One thing I saw early on was that we didn't do a good job of having a transparent, trust-based relationship with our employees. So the trust quotient between the employees and the management was very low. On the other side, the complexity of business was very high. You need to transform, you need to go to emerging markets, you need to drop your price, you need to compete, and for all that, you need employee innovation. In this era of the pink slip, you now have disenchanted employees because of the way you behaved, not with the people you fired, but with the people who remain. You are putting them in uncertain situations, and every time they come to the office, they wonder if a pink slip

> *People don't leave their jobs, they leave their managers.*
>
> *—Dianne Walker*

is waiting. The employee doesn't trust you, and so his or her engagement level at the office is one-tenth of what it could potentially be. You have to create a culture of trust, and that can happen only by pushing the envelope of transparency."

> Focus first on the "why" (as in, the behavior you want to elicit), and much later on the "how much."

Another challenge for leaders today is what Nayar calls the "Facebook culture," in which collaboration is key and the concept of leadership needs to be redefined. "Worldwide, 50 percent of the population is less than 25 years old. For them, who's the leader? There is no leader. They have role models for what is relevant, and everybody has maybe 10 or 15 role models—some in music, some in video, some in social enterprise. So when somebody asks me what kind of a leader I am, I shudder because I don't have the answer. I don't truly believe in the concept called 'omnipresent leader.' Leadership should be finding role models and connecting them with the people who need those role models," Nayar adds.

To lead means to be in charge of the "care and feeding" of those who follow. Care and feeding is not just about the wallet, but, more important, about the soul.

o   Master perpetual encouragement. If it sounds simple, it's not; if it seems obvious, it's elusive.

o   You must win hearts and minds, not buy pocketbooks.

o   Your *attitude* is the organization's *altitude*.

How People Are Paid Influences How They Behave

Studies have shown that employees are more likely to change jobs for career options and training opportunities than for money and benefits, and that seeking opportunities for the long term rather than just the current job has much more influence on job change than monetary compensation. It is not salary that makes a committed employee—money should be seen as a satisfier, but not a driver of employee loyalty. Compensation packages, while important, have become secondary to the employees' desire to be challenged, to contribute, to be recognized, and to know how they will fit into the organization.

> When you're patting someone on the back, let her see your heart.

This is not to claim that pay and benefits are unimportant: there are strong correlations between compensation, benefits plans, and employee commitment. However, the compensation plans with the strongest link to employee commitment are those that give employees a stake in the future success of the organization. Compensation plans in general help to drive commitment when employees understand the plan and believe it to be fair. The way an organization distributes money indicates what management really values, including sending a message to employees as to whether the company truly pays for performance.

In fact, one of the core drivers of HCL's Employees First philosophy is the creation of a performance-driven culture, which makes performance and value creation the cornerstones of the corporate hierarchy—not the power inherent in designation and titles. Compensation, growth, reward, and recognition are all aligned to this primary belief.

"I see a zone of control and a zone of value," Nayar says. "Traditionally, the zone of control—i.e., the managers, the office of the CEO—was very closely linked to the zone of value. The entrepreneur who created the company, he was an engineer, an auditing guy, a manufacturing expert, and everything that happened was linked to his expertise. The guy in control was the guy creating the value. But with the emergence of the knowledge economy, the Internet, emerging global markets, service industries, and business complexity, the zone of control remained where it was: in the CEO's office or with the managers. But the value zone has moved far away, into the interface between customers and employees. Suddenly, you have an organization where the control zone and the value zone are far apart."

I don't care too much for money. Money can't buy me love.

—The Beatles (Lennon/ McCartney)

When Nayar took over as CEO, one of the things his team discovered was that the person who was in control was not actually creating any value. Conversely, the people who were creating value had no control. "So we created what I call a star organization. The control pyramid remains in place because you need it for governance and compensation and important organizational structures. But we also inverted the pyramid, placed it over the control pyramid, and created a star so the people who are creating the value gained control as well. That is the key. HCL's reward and compensation philosophy is aligned to this truth, but at the end of the day compensation is table stakes; it's not the differentiating factor."

Pay must be aligned with the strategy and consistent with the vision. It needs to reinforce the behaviors needed to carry out the strategy. While compensation is not a primary motivator, it does influence behavior. Make sure that compensation reflects reality. People put in sustained efforts to produce the things that get recognized and reinforced.

o   With compensation, focus first on the "why" (as in, the behavior you want to elicit), and much later on the "how much."

o   If people join your organization for money alone, they will leave it for money.

o   Compensation must be competitive. More important than the absolute amount, pay must be equitable within the team.

Different Strokes for Different Folks

Rewarding and celebrating is not one size fits all. Although celebrating accomplishments should be formalized, this needn't always mean a plaque and a party. Informal recognition can be equally sustaining. A handwritten note, sincere words highlighting the difference that someone made, a handshake in the hallway saying, "We couldn't have done it without you," or an e-mail that recognizes effort . . . these are the rewards people that remember the most.

Charles Plumb was a U.S. Navy jet pilot in Vietnam. After 75 combat missions, his plane was destroyed by a surface-to-air missile. Plumb ejected and parachuted into enemy hands. He was captured and spent six years in a Communist Vietnamese prison. He survived the ordeal and now lectures on the lessons he learned from that experience.

One day, when Plumb and his wife were sitting in a restaurant, a man at another table came up and said, "You're Plumb! You flew jet fighters in Vietnam from the aircraft carrier Kitty Hawk. You were shot down!"

"How in the world did you know that?" asked Plumb.

"I packed your parachute," the man replied. Plumb gasped in surprise and gratitude. The man pumped his hand and said, "I guess it worked!"

Plumb assured him, "It sure did. If your chute hadn't worked, I wouldn't be here today."

Plumb couldn't sleep that night, thinking about that man. He says he kept wondering what he had looked like in a Navy uniform: a white hat, a bib in the back, and bell-bottom trousers. He wondered how many times he might have seen him and not even said, "Good morning, how are you?" or anything else because Plumb was a fighter pilot and he was just a sailor. Plumb thought of the many hours the sailor had spent at a long wooden table in the bowels of the ship, carefully weaving the shrouds and folding the silks of each chute, each time holding in his hands the fate of someone he didn't know.

My heart took delight in all my labor, and this was the reward for my toil.
—Ecclesiastes (2:10)

Now, Plumb asks his audiences, "Who's packing your parachute?" Everyone has someone who provides what she needs in order to make it through the day. Plumb also points out that he needed many kinds of parachutes when his plane was shot down over enemy territory: he needed his physical parachute, his mental parachute, his emotional parachute, and his spiritual parachute. He called on all these supports before he reached safety.[2]

In the daily challenges that life gives us, we sometimes miss what is really important. We may fail to say hello, please, or thank you; congratulate someone on something wonderful that has happened to him, give a compliment;, or just do something nice for no reason. As you continue to embark on your mission as a leader, recognize the people who pack your parachutes.

o   Exude sincerity.
o   When you're patting someone on the back, let her see your heart.
o   Meticulously and continuously align goals, expectations, achievements, and rewards.

Everyone Likes a Winner

Winning and pride go hand in hand. Equally important are the way people feel about themselves and the way they are contributing to the journey. Leading means showing pride in both good and not-so-good times—finding the opening in the sky, course correcting the negative, and building on the positive.

We've all worked for—or at least heard stories of—bosses who provide good examples of how *not* to lead people. These are the managers who criticize instead of praise, humiliate and tear down instead of building up and encouraging people to learn from their mistakes. To the misguided, celebrating accomplishments is unnecessary, if not ridiculous. One such story I've heard is that of a sales executive who, upon receiving an e-mail from one of her employees letting her know that he had signed a contract with an important account, responded with the following one-word e-mail reply: "And?" There was no praise, no encouragement, and no acknowledgment. Unfortunately it is not uncommon to find organizations with people in management positions who lack the necessary self-awareness to be effective leaders. Clearly, a culture of reward and celebrate would not tolerate all stick and no carrot; it does not work. People will shut down, tune out, and, when a better opportunity emerges, leave.

> *Victory is won not in miles but in inches. Win a little now, hold your ground, and later, win a little more.*
> —*Louis L'Amour*

At the same time, rewarding and celebrating employees also means that their problems and concerns are important. People won't truly feel cared for if the leader notices only results and fails to acknowledge the challenges that they faced.

At HCL, Nayar explains, a "Smart Service Desk" was created. This desk allows any employee who has a problem to open a trouble ticket on any of the enabling functions. "It is similar to the process we use with customers. The open ticket allows a problem to be tracked from the outset until it is re-solved. By instituting a similar process internally for employees and the enabling functions, we were able to create a trans-parent, efficient system for resolving internal issues. The em-ployee who opened the ticket determines when the problem is sufficiently resolved."

Foster a performance- and achievement-oriented culture by praising not only extraordinary results, but ordinary efforts as well. Demonstrate to people through your words and ac-tions that what people do matters—that you notice, and that you appreciate their efforts.

o   Create opportunity in defeat.
o   Personally and purposefully commit energy and emotion to recognize others.
o   Celebrate often, publicly, and incrementally.

Summary

A leader can build his reputation with employees by using pur-poseful praise—spending a significant amount of time praising workers' specific efforts and actions, and noticing what they're accomplishing. "Thank you; your good work matters today" is an example of a simple statement that builds employee loyalty with the power of praise.

Leaders who manage by walking around are often found to be exceptional motivators of people. They have the pursuit of excellence on their mind when they praise their employees.

They know that striving for excellence demands that they grow the skills of their employees, and that employees grow with the pragmatic power of praise.

Money is a means to an end, not a durable commodity. Making people feel better will stand the test of time. It is so much more enduring to those who hear your praise. Employees work harder for leaders who demonstrate respect for their work. Authentic, purposeful praise is a power skill of the successful leader—everywhere.

CHAPTER 8

ANTICIPATE

It takes as much energy to wish as it does to plan.

—*Eleanor Roosevelt*

magine yourself as a child on a typical long, hot, partly cloudy summer day. You are in the prairie land of Kansas. Between you and the endless horizon are golden, shiny fields of wheat that reaches your shoulders. The day is a scorcher. In the distance are towering, puffy cloud columns that, over time, blanket the afternoon sun. You suddenly feel a cool breeze in the air, followed by a blackening of the sky. The cool breeze finally gives way to an eerie, still calmness. The animals in the grassy field nearby mysteriously start to scamper away for shelter. What do you do? Well, there's one thing for sure: you don't stand under a tree. You know what is going to come next—sonic booms, lightning, hail, and a torrential downpour. You prepare for the worst: a tornado. As the hail hits the barn like a snare drum, you also anticipate the high arc of a rainbow later in the afternoon.

Whether or not you've ever been through this scenario, as I did when I was growing up in Kansas, you can no doubt envision this chain of events. One thing logically leads to the next with the kind of predictability that meteorologists love. Most other things in life, however, are not this obvious, nor will you be able to see the entire horizon. You will need to rely on others who can spot the familiar clouds, and also notice new formations that no one has seen before. As a leader, you need to foster a culture of world-class observers.

As a leader, you need to create the vision, seeing what others cannot. You paint a picture of the future that others cannot yet envision. As you look beyond the next turn in the road, you expect and predict—but you don't guess. You anticipate a future that is grounded in today's reality. You recognize that the seeds of change and challenge are in the here and now. The skill of anticipating is to identify those trends and triggers, and extrapolate their meaning for both the present and the future.

> The better equipped the organization is to see today clearly, the better it will be at systematically predicting the future.

"It really starts with how you view reality," says Warren Bennis, who has devoted his life to leadership. "The leader's job is to get people to look at the present and not just try to read the tea leaves. Then you get everyone to start considering the question: based on what we now know, what are the consequences for us?"

When Bennis speaks, leaders listen. A revered scholar and organizational expert, he has the ear of corporate CEOs and U.S. presidents alike. Much of his career has been devoted to academics. At age 86, he is Distinguished Professor of

Business Administration and founding chairman of the Leadership Institute at the University of Southern California. He is also chairman of the Center for Public Leadership at Harvard's Kennedy School and Distinguished Research Fellow at Harvard Business School. Previously, he served as president of the University of Cincinnati.

It is in the classroom that Bennis is the most at home. At a recent session of his class "The Art and Adventure of Leadership," 42 juniors and seniors (more than 300 had tried to sign up for the class) sat with rapt attention, listening to him relate a story he had read in the *New Yorker* about a small unit of U.S. soldiers who had marched into Naif, a city that houses Iraq's holiest mosque, in January 2005. Soon the soldiers were surrounded by a large and threatening mob. The situation was a powder keg of tension until a young officer held his rifle high above his head and pointed the muzzle downward toward the ground. He ordered the squad to do the same. "Take a knee!" he barked, and the soldiers sank to the ground in a nonthreatening posture. The crowd quieted and then dispersed. For the young officer, the decision as to how to act in that moment was pure intuition.

"The skill of anticipating is critical to leadership, and not just for the leader," Bennis says. "It is essential at every level."

As a leader, you are the steward of tomorrow. But you are not alone. As a leader, you must make anticipating a team sport. Empower others to speak up and share their views about what they see. Perspectives will differ, but that only enriches the discussion. Turn an ordinary team meeting into a session that engages people intellectually and emotionally. Help them to become more conscious of the present and tuned into the future that is unfolding.

"Have members of the team read magazines such as the *Economist* to identify significant events," Bennis advises. "What are the two or three things going on in the world that could have an impact on the organization? Take a phrase such as Arab Spring. What is the meaning of it, and what is its relevance to your organization? Ask team members to write a short summary. Your goal as a leader is to get people to be 'first-class noticers.' It starts with current reality, and then what do you extrapolate from it? What I'm emphasizing really is to make people pay close attention to their current situation."

For the leader, the essential questions to develop the skill of anticipating are: what is happening now, what do these events mean, and what is likely to be the impact on the future? As you answer those questions, you become more comfortable with change—not just reacting to trends, but starting them.

Make the Organization Forward Leaning

The success of your organization will be determined by the accuracy of your intuition and judgment concerning the future: customer needs, competitors' possible countermoves, economic headwinds, employee development, and so forth. Your perception must be grounded in past experience, but not limited by it. The skill of anticipating is grounded in reality, and one of the challenges of a leader is to reconcile the fact that people in the same organization may view reality differently, given their job titles, their backgrounds, and even cultural and language differences. That's particularly the case in a global organization.

"If you look at different levels of the organization, there are many different lenses, including cultural and educational," Bennis says. "The real issue is, how do you get everybody in the organization to be conscious? You need to get people involved. The whole point is, we're not just talking about the world and what they say in foreign affairs magazines, but what are the implications for a leader's particular organization. For example, if you look at the demographic trends in this country and at issues around immigration, you would notice the growing number of Latinos in North America. For an organization like Korn/Ferry, that would mean thinking about identifying potential Latino leaders."

> Leadership is chess—
> think several moves ahead.

Diversity of perspective is to be embraced as an advantage. Every person's viewpoint—his view of reality—is meaningful. When these perspectives are shared, people learn. Once people are looking at reality, a leader's job is to get them to take the next step—from what it means today to what it might mean tomorrow.

"Ask people about a sport they really know about," Bennis says, describing an exercise that can help leaders foster that kind of environment within their organizations. "Would they be able to predict where their favorite teams are going to end up? What is the basis of the prediction: that the team has a good bench? Or is the team going to sink in performance because of a bad coach? How many variables are they going to consider? Maybe the team has the first draft pick or a good farm system. It's not just the Yankees versus the Red Sox, but what are the reasons for one to perform better than the other? The purpose of the exercise is to get people thinking differently. What are the variables? What do those variables mean for us?"

The better equipped the organization is to see today clearly, the better it will be at systematically predicting tomorrow. You don't need the proverbial crystal ball; you need to establish routines and processes that will anchor the organization in real-time data and facts—so that information can bubble up. You and your team need to make the connections and contextualize the data. Then trends can be extrapolated and judgments made.

"There is nothing mysterious about anticipating," Bennis says. "It's about paying attention to the present first—to be able to define reality. What does that

The best laid schemes o' mice and men go oft askew.

—Robert Burns

mean to a business leader? It means one thing: forget about *the* bottom line. There are numerous stakeholders, all of which have a stake in the success or disruption of your business: competitors, vendors, customers, the press, reputation factors."

Anticipate is the skill of looking forward, over the horizon, to see what is not yet clear to others. But the truth is, we can't see the future. If we could, we wouldn't like what we saw. But one of the things a leader has to do is set forth a vision based on what's going to happen in the economy, in the workforce, even with national security. You have to develop a strategy. It's all about making bets on what will happen. Empower others to share what they see, hear, feel, and know.

o   Change the mindset from "this is what we have always done" to "this is what we could do now."

o   Leadership is chess—think several moves ahead.

o   You don't need to be the smartest person in the room, just the most intuitive.

Know What You Don't Know

As the leader, making judgment calls about the future rests squarely on your shoulders. To do so, you need to know what covers the surface of your world. You need not be omnipresent, but you need to be well informed and savvy. Let others be your eyes and ears in places where you cannot see. Empower them to speak up—the consequences of not doing so can often end up being severe.

One extreme example of leaders failing because of their inability to get others involved was a Mount Everest expedition in which a pair of teams encountered grave dangers during their descent from the summit. Each group consisted of the leader, several guides, and eight paying clients. Five individuals, including the two highly talented leaders, Rob Hall and Scott Fischer, died as they tried to climb down the mountain during a stormy night.

Jon Krakauer, a journalist for *Outside* magazine, was a member of Hall's team. The analysis of the calamity that he wrote for *Outside* received a National Magazine Award, and the book he subsequently wrote about Everest, *Into Thin Air*, became a number one *New York Times* bestseller. In it, he wrote about a "guide-client protocol" that began to emerge and shape the climbers' behavior, and that he and the other clients had been "specifically indoctrinated not to question our guides' judgment."

> Set a tone of urgent patience.

For myriad reasons, however, the guides' judgment became skewed in the high-stress environment of trying to overcome extreme elements and reach the peak of the world's highest mountain. In particular, sticking to a predetermined turnaround time—the time at which it would be deemed too late to continue to climb toward the summit and still make it back down to a safe point on the mountain before nightfall brought darkness and even more treacherous weather—was the most important rule of the mountain. "Rob had lectured us repeatedly on this point," Krakauer wrote. "Our turnaround time, he said, would probably be 1 p.m., and no matter how close we were to the top, we were to abide by it."

Unfortunately, the leaders, the guides, and most clients ended up ignoring the turnaround rule. Hall, in fact, didn't start his descent until after 3 p.m., when one of his clients reached the summit. The ensuing blizzard engulfed many climbers during their descent into the darkness. In addition to the five people who died, many others sustained serious injuries, one of which required a client's hand to be amputated because of severe frostbite.

"We were a team in name only, I'd sadly come to realize," Krakauer recounted. "Although in a few hours we would leave camp as a group, we would ascend as individuals, linked to one another by neither rope nor any deep sense of loyalty. Each client was in it for himself or herself."

One of the key breakdowns was that while members certainly recognized the perils associated with violating the turnaround rule, they chose not to question the leaders' judgment. The groups of climbers never had any meaningful conversations with regard to the crucial decision of whether they should continue to forge ahead to reach their goal, or whether they should turn back as had previously been determined.[1]

> *Plan your work for today and every day, then work your plan.*
>
> —*Margaret Thatcher*

"One of the issues with anticipating is getting people to feel free to talk," Bennis says. "It's about listening and encouraging dissenting views. How do you get people to be willing to say, 'I just noticed something,' and to feel free to bring it up? When that happens, people who have never been given the opportunity to express their thoughts will speak up—especially if they are asked to start looking."

Leaders need to embrace such concepts as creating a culture of candor that welcomes the truth, and making anticipate a team sport so that ideas bubble up instead of cascading down. At the same time, anticipating is not perfect. People are going to be wrong. Even if they were right based on the current circumstances, situations can change, both within an organization and globally.

Fortunately, most business decisions are not a matter of life or death. Making the right decisions, however, is vital to an organization's success, and the Mount Everest example stresses the importance of creating a culture of candor, inviting dissenting opinions to enter the discussion. Let experience, knowledge, and intuition be the guides. Pay attention; keep your eyes and ears open, with insatiable curiosity and an appetite for discovery.

o   Information is an equalizer. Foster a culture of information sharing.

o   Always consider the "what ifs" in every scenario.

o   Eliminate the filters between you and the rest of the organization; stay connected to the front line.

o   Know whom to turn to when you need to know more.

Don't Outsource Creativity

As the saying goes, "change is constant"—among your customers, among your competition, and throughout the world. Thus, change must be constant within your organization. You must set the tone not just for change, but change for a purpose through innovation. Encourage continuous idea generation, incubate the promising ideas, and convert the best to define the market.

"Experience is terribly important," Bennis says, "but you cannot be so much in the past that everything is the 'same ol', same ol'.'" Of course your past experiences influence you, but how do you know you are not hostage to the tyranny of stupid theories?"

The Wright brothers, Wilbur and Orville, had always been interested in invention. They designed and built a printing press to publish a newspaper. They opened a bicycle shop and began manufacturing their own brand. The Wrights had another passion, of course: aviation, a nascent field that had attracted visionaries and daredevils, but had not produced success. When a German aviator died in a glider crash, the outcome was tragic, but it showed that manned flight was feasible. The Wright brothers saw the future—and it had wings. Soon Wilbur and Orville were experimenting with gliders on the sand dunes of Lake Michigan. The more they experimented, the more they learned. Anticipating what would make them successful, they sought a place with more wind. The U.S. Weather Bureau provided the data they needed about places in the United States with high wind conditions—places such as Kitty Hawk, North Carolina. During 1900, 1901, and 1902, the Wright brothers experimented with kites, gliders, and

> *Anticipate the difficult by managing the easy.*
>
> —*Lao Tzu*

a wind tunnel that they built to test wing design. Then they made their historic first airplane flight at Kitty Hawk in 1903, followed by several more breakthroughs, including the first flight to last more than an hour, in a demonstration for the U.S. Army in 1908.[2]

Things that are new and different do not materialize out of thin air. People who envision, dream, and anticipate notice what is happening now. They see what others are doing and are determined to try their best. As a leader, you must encourage creativity by allowing new ideas to be explored, even if they never take flight. There is no failure—except failing to try.

o   You'll never cut your way to growth. Invest in tomorrow.

o   Inspire and celebrate the new and different.

o   Set a tone of urgent patience. Creativity takes time—but not too much of it.

Stay Lean

For your organization, there will undoubtedly be periods of adversity—a figurative winter when it seems better to hibernate than to venture out. Resist that urge. These are the times when companies can make their best moves, assuming that they were stewards of their resources during better times. Beware the summer, though.

Our goals can only be reached through a vehicle of a plan, in which we must fervently believe, and upon which we must vigorously act. There is no other route to success.

—Pablo Picasso

Good times are deceptively deadly; they can cover a multitude of sins and breed complacency. As a leader, you must continually challenge, rather than question. Keep the organization hungry and lean so that it can maneuver like a Jet Ski rather than a supertanker.

"We need to sustain growth, not just sustain what has come before so that we're living with the past," Bennis says. "Sustainability also has the implication not just of sustaining business, but of sustaining growth. This is very related to anticipate."

As we look at the news and the buzzwords of today, obviously the main concerns in this country are economic growth and jobs. President Obama has to show compassion and energy concerning whether we are going to create jobs in the future at the rate that we did in the past. The first decade of the twenty-first century was a lost decade in terms of job creation—no net new jobs were created in those 10 years, and this may continue for a total of 15 years. It's all about growth and innovation—but it's also about shared sacrifice as well.

"There has to be some amount of buy-in—not consensus, but buy-in," Bennis says. "That's what people want. Shared sacrifice is important. Young people, especially, want to be called on. More and more students, among USC's best, have a 'save the world' attitude. The nongovernmental organizations (NGOs) and not-for-profits have more appeal today than [they did] when I first started teaching my leadership courses at USC in 1995. That has been increasing. More graduates today go to Teach America [which recruits recent college graduates and professionals from all backgrounds to teach in low-income communities for two years]. This reflects the theme of shared sacrifice."

Bennis' comments brought to my mind one day in the spring of 2010 when I spent a few hours with Carlos Slim, an entrepreneur who had deliberately kept a low profile until, just a few weeks before our meeting, his name appeared at the top of the Forbes list of billionaires. Although I was sitting with the world's richest person, that was not what struck me about our time together. In fact, for most of our conversation, the subject of wealth came up only tangentially, in the context of what Slim saw as the obligation to deploy money like any resource: to improve society, such as creating private-sector jobs and opportunities for others. In our conversation, Slim shared his approach to business and his belief that the best time to invest is when others are panicking. Like his father before him, who invested during times of crisis and economic uncertainty in the last century, Slim patiently buys when others are rushing to sell, such as during the financial crisis of 2008.

The lesson learned from Slim was not just about bargain hunting. The bigger takeaway from Slim's experience was the power of anticipating the future: when growth would resume, and when and where shell-shocked consumers would resume their spending habits. These opportunities, however, go only to those who are most prepared—to the ones who have been diligent and disciplined during the good days in order to survive and thrive during the lean ones.

- Always have a backup plan—and a backup for the backup.
- Recognize that the figurative winter is for investing; summer is for saving. When times are good and cash is coming in, don't spend away your future.
- Rely on your experience, but always listen to your intuition.
- "Push" during better times; "pull" during tougher times.

Summary

As a leader, you must always have your focus on the horizon. Where is the economy headed? What will your market or industry look like? What will your competitors do? What is your plan of action—and your countermove?

"Think of what happens in Korn/Ferry's business," Bennis says. "You find the most qualified candidates, but will they be successful? A lot depends upon exogenous factors—on the economy, government intervention, health, changes in technology and social media. When someone whom you think has all the right stuff is placed in a job, even if he or she is perfect, even then there is no guarantee."

> Make anticipating a team sport.

Anticipating will never be reduced to a science. You must use your intuition as well as your intellect. Anticipating involves reviewing alternatives and acting decisively when others only observe. It must engage others to observe the events of today—economic, social, and political—and extrapolate both their meaning and their impact on tomorrow.

The skill of anticipating is the art of looking ahead, starting from where you are—right here, right now. Your first task is to hone your view of the present that you perceive around you and your organization. Grounded in this reality, you are able to raise your sights toward the horizon and beyond.

CHAPTER 9

NAVIGATE

*By prevailing over all obstacles and
distractions, one may unfailingly arrive
at his chosen goal or destination.*
                    —Christopher Columbus

C oupled with anticipate, the skill of navigate
is the essence of strategic thinking, and even
more so today than at any time in the past, giv-
en how rapidly the world is changing. Navigating takes objectivity and clarity to see opportunities, honesty to admit mistakes, and courage
to make real-time decisions toward a new way forward. When
you navigate, setting strategy is not a once-a-year exercise. It
becomes perpetual in the form of thoughtful and proactive decision making in the midst of a changing environment. Yet a
leader must be mindful of the difference between the urgent
and the important, the tactical and the strategic.

Few executives understand what this means in today's
fast-paced business environment better than Jeff Weiner, the
CEO of the professional networking site LinkedIn.com, which
in 2011 passed the 130 million member mark. As anyone who
has ever received a "join my professional network" invitation

knows, LinkedIn is not your average post-your-résumé site. Its average member is said to be a college-educated 43-year-old making $107,000 a year, and more than a quarter of its members are senior executives.

"When an organization is growing very quickly, you want to make sure that you stay as focused as possible," Weiner says. "You really start with your core. Visualize a target—and every target has a bull's-eye. Companies will have a far greater likelihood of being successful in achieving their mission if they have a clear sense of what that bull's-eye is, because they can always make sure that's where the first dollar of investment goes, where the first managerial cycle goes. That's the first priority. And I think that clear sense of mission is important because it will heavily influence your strategy."

LinkedIn's defining focus is to connect talent with opportunity at massive scale. Its strategy is to carry out that mission while offering new resources to represent professional identity, provide valuable insights, and work wherever their members work. While never losing sight of its purpose or its strategy, LinkedIn must be responsive and nimble as opportunities arise or the competitive landscape shifts. Only by constantly measuring its progress can the company determine if it is still on course or if its trajectory has been altered.

What lies behind us and what lies before us are tiny matters compared to what lies within us.

—*Ralph Waldo Emerson*

"The strategy is designed such that we can measure our ability to execute against it," Weiner says. "We understand our competitive landscape. We are always keeping our eyes and ears open for the progress we're making in terms of realizing strategic objectives, and how the landscape is evolving so that we can make course corrections in real time."

Navigating Is Decision Making

As the CEO of LinkedIn, which was founded in 2002 and officially launched in 2003, Weiner seeks out new growth opportunities, such as in emerging markets. A 17-year veteran of Internet businesses and a former executive vice president at Yahoo!, Weiner knows well the agility needed to navigate in a fast-moving industry.

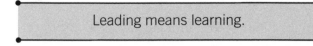

Leading means learning.

"Our mission is to connect the world's professionals to make them more productive and successful," Weiner says. "That's what we do, and that's what we measure. There are as many as half a billion professionals in the world, and we think that number is going to grow along with the developing economies of the world. We understand our strategic objectives, we understand our landscape, and we are monitoring and collecting the right data and insights to make sure we can make the right course corrections as we go. The vision is to create economic opportunity for every professional in the world. Broadly defined, there are as many as 3.3 billion people in the global workforce. We want to be able to reach them all."

Navigating in a hypergrowth, real-time world means continually getting people back on course. Although course corrections will occur, the focus must always stay on the opportunities that will increase the likelihood of success. As Weiner observes, "The degree of difficulty goes up as you try to execute more and more things. A wonderful analogy an old friend of mine used is that if you are about to launch a rocket and that launch trajectory is off by even inches, the rocket is going to be off by miles out in orbit. Mission is what starts that trajectory. Strategy and navigation are what enable you to stay focused on maintaining that trajectory over time."

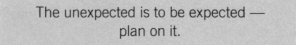

The unexpected is to be expected —
plan on it.

To be a leader is to anticipate what is coming down the road—always being prepared, responsive, and forward-thinking. The ability to navigate is a complementary skill, involving making decisions in real time that allow you to adjust, react, and outmaneuver the competition.

The New England Patriots' fifteenth offensive play of the 2008 season drastically altered the course for a team that had been chosen by most to win the Super Bowl following a season in which they had come up 35 seconds short of being the first team ever to go 19-0. On the field, quarterback Tom Brady was the undisputed star of the team, setting an NFL regular-season record with 50 touchdown passes en route to league MVP honors. His supporting cast for the 2008 season remained almost entirely intact.

When Brady was injured, however, the team had to play without him. It was up to Patriots head coach Bill Belichick to lead his team through the remaining 98.5 percent of the season on a course far different from the one that had been set over months of off-season workouts, training camp, and pre-season games. The offense had to change hands from Brady, the NFL's best player, to Matt Cassel, who had last started a football game as quarterback nine years previously, in 1999—for the Chatsworth High School Chancellors. The fact that the mighty Patriots would be underdogs in Cassel's first start—against a Jets team that had won a total of four games the previous year—sums up the extremely low expectations that fans and experts had for the Cassel-led Patriots.

What people underestimated was Belichick's keen ability to navigate the rough seas that had knocked his team so drastically off course. As the leader—the captain of the ship—Belichick realized that he needed to be present in the moment to outmaneuver the storm—even when injuries threatened to ruin a season that the coach and his team had tried so hard to rescue.

> *If one tries to navigate unknown waters one runs the risk of shipwreck.*
>
> —*Albert Einstein*

Following two heartbreaking, extremely close losses at the hands of two of their biggest rivals (the Colts and the Jets), no one would have blamed the Patriots if they had lost their focus and begun looking to next year. But Belichick never stopped charting new courses to overcome the obstacles that were put in his team's way. The Patriots went on to finish their season with an impressive four-game winning streak to leave their record at an astoundingly impressive 11-5, tied for the best record in their division and the fifth-best record in the entire NFL. In a season in which his team suffered injuries that would probably have crippled most other franchises, Belichick maintained his focus and got the very most out of his team.[1]

The lessons of the gridiron apply to the corporate arena as well. You need to have a balance between agility and adjustment, while maintaining forward momentum. The key is having metrics that flag outlying risks and draw attention to issues as they arise. Your team should also know that, if needed, you are only a phone call, an e-mail, or a few doors away.

o   Plan a little; think a lot; decide always.

o   Problems are opportunities in waiting.

o   Ensure that "investment" is not a code word for poor decisions. Have expectations for every undertaking, and measure progress.

o   Never allow success to breed complacency.

Rise above the Unexpected

It has been said that one can choose to avoid reality, but one cannot avoid the consequences of avoiding reality. Sometimes reality will offer a type of adversity that you simply cannot navigate around. Your only choice is to act, to put a difficult reality behind you, to make it history. Effective leaders meet conflict head on and resolve it constructively, decisively, and on a timely basis.

"Once the strategy is put in place based on what you anticipate, annual and biannual strategic planning processes are no longer sufficient," Weiner says. "You have to be able to move much faster than that. We live in real time—with real-time media and information distribution. Consequently, you've got to be ready to respond and navigate in real time. That's a very different mindset and requires a different approach and perspective."

As a leader, you must engage in constant checking. This requires high-touch feedback gathered from and delivered to your team: what is going well, and what can be done better. With navigating, there are no secrets. Information is shared so that everyone on the team knows where she is, where she is going, and what is up ahead.

> Plan a little, think a lot, decide always.

"We are completely transparent in terms of what we're up to, against our key corporatewide priorities and our strategic objectives," Weiner says. "We do an all-hands meeting here every other week so that the company can see how we're performing. We use that meeting as an opportunity to share successes and, perhaps more important, what's not working. We talk about what we can learn from that and how we can course-correct. When you are transparent like that, you accrue great benefits, because people have visibility into what's moving the needle, into what works and what doesn't. The all-hands meeting is a big part of how we establish trust."

The ability to navigate in real time keeps a leader agile in the moment, yet always focused on the horizon. I draw a parallel to surfing, a sport that I'm taking up with my son, Jack. This is quiet time for us, out on the ocean in the early morning hours, with no distractions such as iPhones and BlackBerries. For a surfer, it's all about focus and balance. Once you pick your wave in the moment and you're up on the board, you absolutely have to look straight ahead to the horizon. If you look down, you will fall.

The same is true for a leader. To navigate, you have to choose the opportunities that are presented in the moment, the "wave" that will bring you that much closer to your goal. You can't become so focused on the here and now, however, that you lose your balance. Look to the horizon to keep the forward momentum that will take you where you need to be.

> *I have not failed. I've found 10,000 ways that won't work.*
>
> *—Thomas Edison*

"When I first became an executive with broader responsibility, before my current CEO role, my tendency was to fly at a lower altitude because I was more in execution mode," Weiner says. "So one of the things I learned was to not be only in the weeds, because I think that's a natural tendency for someone who has gained more responsibility. I've incorporated that learning where I try to operate at a higher altitude. At the same time, I need to understand how we're executing—knowing when to get more involved in the day-to-day; when to start course-correcting when something isn't going as well as it otherwise might; when to make a move in terms of key talent in a key role. I found you can't always assume that things are going a certain way in the day-to-day operations. You need to make sure that you're taking the pulse of the organization periodically and [that you] understand how things are going without making assumptions."

The crucial takeaway for leaders is, never lose sight of the larger strategy when you're making tactical decisions; never be so removed that the results of tactical decisions become de facto strategy. Navigating keeps you constantly in touch with your customers and with the marketplace. You are a world-class observer, objectively and continually measuring and interpreting the results of today to make decisions tomorrow.

"A great axiom that a colleague of mine likes to say is, 'If you can't measure it, you can't fix it,'" Weiner says. "So our ability to measure what we're doing and our realization of our execution against certain priorities becomes critical. We measure in real time because we operate in real time. You can't have your consumers consuming products and services on one time dimension and the company operating on another. That disconnect is going to create too much dissonance."

o   Failure to choose is a choice.

o   Leadership means rising above.

o   Keep your eyes on the horizon, but stay grounded.

Admit Mistakes

No one is infallible. Human beings and organizations will make mistakes. It's an uncomfortable but unavoidable truth: leading means learning. As a leader, your learning is exponential.

"We course-correct as we go, so that's a big part of navigation," Weiner says. "Another big part of it is the things occurring outside of our company—so it's paying close attention to the right signposts. How is the landscape evolving? How is the industry evolving? How is technology changing what is possible? How is innovation changing products and services that our customers have come to rely on? What moves is the competition making? What moves are noncompetitive companies making that we can learn from or benefit from? And then we have the right tools in place to separate the signal from the noise."

> Failure to choose is a choice.

As leaders well know, many innovations fail, many proposals fail, and many efforts to bring about change fail. Anything that is worth doing takes repeated effort. Admit the mistakes, analyze what went wrong, learn the lessons, and move forward decisively.

"Continuous improvement is a huge part of what we do," Weiner says. "By collecting the data and the business intelligence, we're able to understand where we're successful and where we need to improve. We learn from both, our successes as well as our failures."

Those who fail to learn this lesson are doomed to reap the consequences. Consider this story: Company X had just completed a CEO succession process. As the former CEO left the building, he said to his successor, "If you ever get into trouble, check your top desk drawer." Six months later, the company's sales stalled. As the new CEO wondered what he should do, he remembered his predecessor's parting message. Opening his top desk drawer, he discovered three envelopes. Written on the outside of one envelope were the words, "In the event of

A crisis is an opportunity riding the dangerous wind.
—Chinese proverb

trouble, open this envelope first." Eagerly the CEO tore the envelope open and looked inside. On a plain piece of paper were the words, "Blame your predecessor."

He took that advice to heart in a conference call with Wall Street analysts who were questioning the CEO about the decline in sales. Blaming his predecessor worked very well, and people responded favorably.

After another six months, things worsened. The CEO went back to his desk drawer and took out the second envelope. Inside was a one-word message: "Restructure." So a major reorganization was announced. Analysts and investors responded well, and the stock recovered. Then, a year later, sales plummeted again. Discouraged, the CEO opened the third and last envelope. Inside, the message read: "Prepare three envelopes."

There is no real failure except the failure to learn from one's mistakes. Excuses and blame may buy you a little time, but in the end, they will do more harm than good. Accept responsibility, correct your course if necessary, and learn from what went wrong.

o   It's not failure; it's called learning.
o   Decision making in the here and now shouldn't steal from the future. Keep a forward focus.

o   Transparency is always the best policy.

o   When you are a leader, failure is your responsibility. Accept it and move on. Blame is an insidious poison that tears teams apart.

Know When to Take the Wheel

For leaders, not a day goes by without someone saying, "I don't need to bother you with that"—as if, in some way, the issue or its details are beneath you. As a leader, you are responsible for the totality of the organization. You own 35,000 feet, but you must understand the entire airspace. Nothing should be "beneath" you.

"Sometimes people can hit their numbers, but they're still not doing things in a way that is constructive or in the best long-term interest of the company," Weiner says. "So you need to carve out the time to focus on the day-to-day to make sure things are consistent with the way you've set up your overarching objectives and the culture and values of an organization, and then enable people to do their thing. You're not going to have the time to do it as often as you need to because you're going to prioritize and you're going to want to assume from time to time that things are going the way you wanted them to go, that culturally people are operating consistently with the culture of the organization, that you've got the right person in the right role. That's one reason why we use key performance indicators and key metrics—so we can track that."

How and when you need to take the wheel depends upon the organization and the circumstances. I can remember riding my bike down the street in a small Kansas town in July 1969 and hearing the words projected out of the screen door of a house: "The Eagle has landed!" As I kept riding, I heard cheers coming from another house. All day long, people talked about the magical thing that had just happened: men had landed on the moon. Years later, I learned that this historic moment also serves as one of the most dramatic examples of a leader taking the wheel.

> Your confidence becomes others' assurance.

As the lunar landing module known as the Eagle neared the surface of the moon (the ultimate uncharted territory!), it was fully under the control of a computerized guidance system. For astronauts Neil Armstrong and Buzz Aldrin, it was supposed to be a totally hands-off operation. Moments before touchdown, however, Armstrong noticed that the targeted landing site was at the edge of a large crater surrounded by boulders. Realizing the danger, Armstrong made the split-second decision to override the computer and land the Eagle manually, with only 30 seconds' worth of fuel left. With the Eagle safely on the surface of the moon, Armstrong calmly sent a message to Mission Control: "The Eagle has landed."[2]

Similarly, leaders must know when to take the wheel and guide the organization through rough terrain to safer ground. To accomplish that, leaders must stay close to the action.

"When I'm walking the floor, I try to make a point of talking to different teams," Weiner says. "We have very open floor space here, which is an important part of creating a collaborative environment. When you get folks talking about what they're working on and what gets them excited, you get the energy going. Pretty soon, it'll attract a few more people. Sometimes those meetings can be the most valuable in terms of taking the pulse of the organization. I also have an open-door policy. Everyone at the company knows that as long as I'm in my office and I'm not meeting somebody else, they can come in and share whatever is on their minds. It's always been like that, and it always will be like that."

As a leader receives all of these data and input—both metrics that measure things in real time and feedback from his team—he must decide how to filter it. One of the keys is being able to separate and differentiate between the urgent and the important.

"You have to delegate— which requires the right people on your team—or you won't have time to coach," Weiner says. "You're not going to have the time to think proactively. You're not going to have the

I skate to where the puck is going to be, not where it has been.

—Wayne Gretzky

time to think strategically. You'll be constantly reacting to your circumstances. In a highly competitive industry, that's going to lead to real problems because you'll end up chasing the competition instead of leading the competition. More often than not, you'll replicate the competition instead of playing your own game."

The more critical the issue, the more the leader is likely to hover at ground level with a hand on the control. With an empowered team to which the leader can delegate, however, a

CEO is able to own the upper airspace, swooping down to the ground only as needed.

"When someone comes to you with a problem, the natural inclination is to roll up your sleeves and try to fix it," Weiner says. "Instead, take the time to understand what that person is best at, how he or she got into the situation, whether or not it's systemic, and not only how you can address that situation, but also how that individual can learn to proactively avoid that situation if it's a problem—or how to replicate the success if it's something that has exceeded expectations."

o   Seek to understand, not to blame. Group problem solving is empowering; problem hiding is a recipe for disaster.

o   When a crisis hits, courage counts the most. You can't know the right answer, but you can be informed, consider alternatives, and act decisively.

o   Your confidence becomes others' assurance.

Summary

"Feedback from your team is an important form of measurement," Weiner says. "Establish a culture that is open, honest, and constructive—and I use the word *constructive* very purposefully, because you can be open and honest without being constructive."

While you are the captain of your ship, you need to have confidence in the members of your crew. Empower them to keep a watchful eye out for rocks and shoals, or for a fortuitous shift in the winds. Let them take the wheel while you take out the charts and set the course for the farthest reaches.

"Create an environment where people feel comfortable sharing—and not just what's working, because that's easy," Weiner says. "Let's celebrate the wins. Let's talk about the things that we're doing right. But [people should] feel equally comfortable talking about what's not working. I think to some extent that's even more important, because how else are you going to grow and get better and improve an organization? Creating an environment and a culture of collaboration where we are constantly reinforcing this openness, this honesty, and this constructiveness is how we can get insight and visibility into the things we can be doing better. That's how you can navigate your course to be on a path of continuous improvement. That's how you build a world-class organization."

As a leader, although you do not have a complete view of the future, you must define it through navigation and action—in other words, through decision making. Navigation happens in the moment, with adjustments in speed, altitude, and direction as needed. Keep an eye on the ground, but never lose sight of the horizon. No matter how well you plan and anticipate, the unexpected is to be expected—plan on it.

CHAPTER 10

COMMUNICATE

*Think like a wise man but
communicate in the language of
the people.*

—*William Butler Yeats*

F
or a leader, communication is connection and inspiration—not just transmission of information.
Communication is critical for building alignment
and executing strategy. Yet it is often one of the most
challenging leadership skills because it is so easy to
say, but not so easy to do. Effective communication
is far more than a one-way street that starts with the leader.
Communication is the leader's "information highway"; it flows
freely in both directions and in every circumstance—in good
times and, especially, in challenging ones.

Whether spoken or written, and spanning both words and
actions, the message must always convey both your vision and
the organization's purpose and values. What too many people
fail to fully appreciate is that the message is not just what you
say; how you say it is equally important. Communication is
where leadership lives and breathes.

For Angela Ahrendts, an American midwesterner (and proud of it) who is CEO of Burberry Group plc, communication was her number one commitment from her first day on the job five years ago. At that time, she and chief creative officer Christopher Bailey pledged to communicate "very clearly, very consistently, and very openly" with employees so that they understood and embraced the company's strategic direction. In fact, the very first meeting that Ahrendts and Bailey had with employees was a live Webcast, during which they laid out a strategy to leverage the Burberry franchise—its brand, including its signature outerwear and its iconic check plaid.

"We said, 'Communication is the only way that we can connect.' Connect is such a big word. At that point in time, we had 5,000 employees around the world; there are 7,000 today. We asked ourselves, 'How do we share with them? How do we communicate? How do we touch them in the most effective, most clear way, and on a very consistent basis?' We needed to be very, very clear on what we wanted to do," Ahrendts explained.

> *Words mean more than what is set down on paper. It takes the human voice to infuse them with deeper meaning.*
>
> —*Maya Angelou*

The Leader Is the Message

Sharing information is critical, but it is substantially less than half the battle. Yes, you must communicate clearly about the organization's strategy, speed, direction, and results. But you cannot stop there. Verbally and nonverbally, the way in which you communicate—humbly, passionately, confidently—has more impact than the words you choose.

As a leader, you must inspire others through your words and actions. And before you speak, make sure you listen and observe; knowing your audience is as important as the message you're delivering. Communication informs, persuades, guides, and assures, as well as inspires. You must be willing to reveal more of yourself, to let others see your soul. If you don't, you will undermine your effectiveness as a leader, and your followers may soon drift to the sidelines.

> In good times, people look to the leader for validation, and in difficult times they look to the leader for assurance.

"I think that the larger and more complex the business gets, I have to listen twice as much as I speak," Ahrendts says. "The sign of a great leader is knowing what you know and knowing what you don't know. I probably say that once a day. And I remind my team, and myself, too, that [no matter how] large and successful we get, we can't lose our objectivity—ever. I always say that my job is not to think about today. My job is to look around the corner and feel and see what's coming, and then warn everybody else."

As I shared in the opening chapter, when I first became CEO, I was so concerned with the content of my message that I failed to appreciate that my tone of voice, my facial expression, and my body language—all of these things—were as much the message as the words I spoke. Why? Because humans are intuitive. We constantly read and react to nonverbal cues. As the leader, I had to be aware at all times of what I was projecting to others, whether they saw me as confident and optimistic or tentative and worried. Of all the responsibilities of leadership, particularly during challenging times, communication is the most powerful and enduring.

Ahrendts's approach and the way she communicates reflect who she is and where she came from. She credits the Golden Rule of "do unto others" that she learned from her parents—her father, "the philosopher," and her mother, "who had very strong faith," as she describes them. "I was raised with very strong core values," Ahrendts says. "Ninety-five percent of the time, I put myself in somebody else's position—that's how I live. I've been in a lot of situations in my life, and regardless, I've always relied on those values to keep me strong and to keep my confidence."

> Back up what you say with what you do.

The alternative is to ignore the ground rules of communication and shut down the two-way flow of information. Consider the story of a new CEO. At his first town hall meeting with employees, he took to the podium with a command-and-control style that showed that there was a new sheriff in town and things were going to change. With hundreds of employees in the audience, the CEO began speaking. Suddenly, he noticed a man in the corner of the room who wasn't paying attention to him. Furthermore, the man wasn't dressed like the rest of the audience; he was in jeans and a T-shirt, with a baseball cap on sideways. Here was a perfect example, the CEO thought to himself, to show employees that such laxity was not going to be permitted.

"You in the corner," the CEO yelled out. "How much do you make a week?" Looking up in surprise, the guy replied that he made about $400 a week. With a smirk, the CEO reached into his pocket and pulled out about $1,000 in cash. "You're fired!" he said. As the man in the baseball cap took the money, the CEO noticed the funny grin on his face, but he ignored it. Some of the employees were smiling; others seemed stunned. No matter, the CEO told himself; he'd made his point.

> *The superior man acts before he speaks, and afterwards speaks according to his action.*
>
> —*Confucius*

After his speech, the CEO called one of his lieutenants over. "So, how do you think I did?" he asked. "I sure made an example of that guy. By the way, who was he?"

"That was Johnny the pizza delivery guy. He was bringing us lunch, and he sure appreciated the tip you gave him."

Before you speak, know your audience. Listen and ask questions. Notice the nonverbal cues, and pay attention to people's reactions, facial expressions, gestures, and mood. Otherwise, you could be communicating the wrong message to the wrong people.

o   It is not only what you say, but how you say it.

o   What you say reverberates throughout the organization. What you don't say may echo even more.

o   For a leader, there are no off-the-cuff remarks.

o   Communication informs, persuades, guides, and assures, as well as inspires. You must be willing to reveal more of yourself, to let others see your soul.

Communicate—or Else Drown Others in Uncertainty

One of the most important skills for any leader is the ability to communicate—not only to convey information, but also to inspire and guide. In good times, people look to the leader for validation, and in difficult times, they look to the leader for assurance. People would rather know the truth about a difficult situation, not dwell in their imagination's worst-case scenarios.

For Burberry, one of those difficult times was the financial crisis of 2008. "We were halfway there on the strategy when the market started to drop," Ahrendts says. "We needed to cut £50 million of expenses out of the business. To convey this message, I had to go back to my core values. How do you do this as if someone were doing it to you? I told them I was scared to death, but we were all in this together. I told them what I thought and what we should do."

Ahrendts and her team had communicated the same message to the board of directors, including an action plan to reduce unnecessary expenses. A cross-collaborative team was put together, and a one-week deadline for identifying a list of inefficiencies was set. Her strategy worked; because she had had the courage to communicate the extent of the problem and the confidence to present a solution, Ahrendts gained the buy-in of the team. "If you have a trusting relationship and people feel empowered, they will do what needs to be done," she adds.

As a leader, if you don't communicate, you will be the subject of communication—and not in a flattering way. The people whom you expect to have following you, in total alignment with the purpose and strategy of the organization, will instead spend their time speculating. Why? Because your lack of sufficient communication has left a vacuum that others will fill.

> You do not speak for yourself. Rather, you speak on behalf of the entire organization.

A lack of information, if not addressed, usually leads to hazardous uncertainty. Human beings can deal with certainty no matter what the outcome, but uncertainty breeds conjecture, resulting in fear and chaos. In the event of the unexpected, explain what happened. Nip uncertainty and speculation in the bud. Communicate to fill the void, to express intent— yours and the organization's. Be consistent in your message. Then back up what you say with what you do.

"In the case of the downturn [in 2008], the biggest part of the layoffs and the cost cuts came out of one particular market that had been a licensed market," Ahrendts says. "It wasn't a massive layoff across the company. Nonetheless, everybody was afraid. I came in the following morning and told the CFO and the head of marketing, 'We're going to do a Webcast today.' And then I talked to all the employees. I told them, 'You know, we've been through things before, but none of us have ever been through anything like this before. We have to batten down the hatches. We're going into one hell of a storm, and together we can do this.' We didn't talk about cutting £50 million of expenses. We said we're going to have to cut £50 million of inefficiencies out of the business. What I said was, 'Let's take the opportunity to do things differently.'"

Through your communication, you establish credibility. Wherever and whenever possible, share information openly and equally with all parties. If you can't do so, explain why. Resist the urge to soften or distort uncomfortable messages. People will notice, and it will undermine your credibility in the long run.

One of the most powerful examples of using communication to empower others is Wael Ghonim. An executive for Google in charge of marketing in the Middle East and North Africa, he established an anonymous Facebook page in honor of a young Egyptian who had been tortured to death by the police. Within six months, the "We Are All Khaled Said" page had nearly 500,000 members. (As of mid-2011, it had 1.5 million "like" endorsements.) The page was more than just a tribute; it became a tool for organizing protests against the Mubarak government in Egypt.

In the last analysis, what we are communicates far more eloquently than anything we say or do.
—Stephen Covey

Using the viral power of social media, Ghonim catalyzed change in his country and helped to inspire the "Arab Spring" of pro-democracy protests across the region. Time magazine, which named Ghonim as one of the 100 most influential people of 2011, noted, "What Wael and the young Egyptians did spread like wildfire across the Arab world." [1]

Never underestimate the power of one voice. When disseminated broadly, communication sparks a course of action for many.

o   Counter fear with facts and hope.

o   Communicate all the facts, but not until you have all the facts. When the information you have is incomplete, state what you can and tell people when you will be able to tell them more.

o   You do not speak for yourself. Rather, you speak on behalf of the entire organization.

Welcome the Truth

If you want the truth, you must welcome it—on that, every leader agrees. Even Mao Tse-Tung observed, "Unless the principle of 'don't blame the speaker' is observed genuinely and not falsely, the result will not be 'Say all you know and say it without reserve.'" As the leader, you set the tone through your attentiveness, attitude, and body language. In the case of speaking, you must receive more than you give. When you receive honest feedback from your team, you may not like what you hear. If so, then congratulations—you've engendered enough trust that people are willing to tell you what they really think and not what they think you want to hear.

Not receiving honest feedback from your team can often lead to disastrous results. One extreme example of this is the tragedy of the space shuttle Columbia, which disintegrated over Texas during reentry into the Earth's atmosphere on February 1, 2003, resulting in the death of all seven crew members. The loss of the Columbia was a result of damage sustained during launch, when a piece of foam insulation the size of a small briefcase broke off from the space shuttle's external tank. According to the 248-page report filed months later by the Columbia Accident Investigation Board, the loss of the Columbia was also the result of, among other things, poor communication throughout the NASA organization.

The disaster, the report said, was fully rooted in a flawed NASA culture that downplayed risk and suppressed dissent. The space shuttle engineers, who desperately wanted zoom-in satellite pictures of the damaged Columbia in orbit, never spoke up at key meetings and never told the manager in charge of the flight. They were too afraid, largely because of a culture that had been created under a previous NASA boss, who reportedly intimidated many workers with his abrasive, demanding demeanor. Because of the culture, critical messages were not shared with the right people, and tragedy occurred.[2]

> The wise ones fashioned speech with their thought, sifting it as grain is sifted through a sieve.
>
> —Buddha

Honor the knowledge experts on your team and throughout the organization by seeking out their input and their opinions. Those who are closer to the front lines will have a different perspective and will probably know more about the details of what is happening than you do. By engaging in dialogue—speaking with and listening to others—you raise the confidence and competence of your team.

At times the messages may come to you indirectly. At a recent employee gathering at Korn/Ferry, for example, a few people joked with me about their not having received a gift for their 10-year anniversary with the company, something that had been done in the past. The remarks were offhand and jovial, but I could hear the truth behind the comments. Some of them wondered why the practice had stopped; others were genuinely upset but tried to hide it. My job was to take it all in and to respond appropriately. How I felt at the moment was immaterial. If I want to hear all the truth, I have to create a safe environment that welcomes it. That means managing my emotional reactions.

Watch your verbal and nonverbal cues so that you don't appear agitated, annoyed, or angry because of the feedback you're hearing. Reflect and then respond.

- When your team members believe they can trust what you say, they will follow what you do.
- Engender trust, that "what's said here stays here."
- Exude fairness. Favoritism and judgments (perceived or real) undermine your credibility.
- Ensure that people talk openly based on fact, not on uninformed opinion. When they do, truth happens.
- Intersect "your" view and "my" view to create trust.

Communication Is Not Talking to Hear Yourself Think

You already know what you think. Just because you're the leader doesn't mean that you do all the talking. In fact, true leaders do far more listening than talking. Speak with purpose, talking with the team rather than to the team. If knowledge is power, then empower your team with information.

"We talked early on about what would be our legacy back to this great brand," Ahrendts says. "We told our teams that if we have these heritage icons, it's not about ubiquity, it's not about price. It's about protecting; it's about coveting. So phase one of the check was that we just started cleaning [how it was used]—taking it off everything because it had become almost ubiquitous instead of being protected or coveted like a historic icon should be."

> When your team members believe they can trust what you say, they will follow what you do.

The problem with communication is that it takes time—and lots of it. The temptation, therefore, is to take shortcuts, such as assuming that people already know certain information, or else glossing over a message from an employee or passing it along to someone else. When you take the time to acknowledge an e-mail or written note from an employee, even with a few words, you've immediately conveyed that you care and that the other person matters.

"When people send me an e-mail, they know I read everything—even if they don't get a response," Ahrendts says. "But 90 percent of the time, they do. It's very easy to say, 'Thanks,' or 'Fabulous, thanks.' Just simple responses—you don't have to write paragraphs for everything."

Ahrendts's effective communication style was one of the keys to Burberry's being able to weather the heavy storm that was the financial crisis of 2008. We saw firsthand evidence of this when we visited the Burberry store on Wilshire Boulevard in Beverly Hills and talked to the manager. When we mentioned that we were going to see Ahrendts, the store manager spoke as if he knew everything about her. A store employee came over and engaged in the dialogue as well. Clearly that stems from her open relationship with employees. I don't think there are a lot of other organizations in which people feel that connected to the person sitting in the CEO's office.

"If we wanted to be a great luxury brand, then we needed to behave like a great luxury brand," Ahrendts says. "So part of writing a 'new chapter' for the company was opening a new headquarters in London. We built a living, breathing vision of the brand so that anybody who walked in could feel it immediately. We have a lot of new people coming into the company. We moved 500 people into the [London] building two years ago. There are 1,100 here today. That's the growth of the company. So how do you bring in so many new people and

> *Wise men speak because they have something to say; fools because they have to say something.*
>
> —*Plato*

get them to feel the culture and understand the culture? We have a pretty good onboarding program now. All the Webcasts that we do, anything we communicate, are on video that they can see. When new people start now, they go through a week of understanding the company and understanding our values."

Communication is connecting and engaging with others. Deliver your message frequently and consistently, with candor and honesty. As a leader, you must speak with more assurance than authority. Be as concerned with your tone as with your content.

"We share with investors that we will continue to grow the top and the bottom lines, but we still have some legacy issues that we have to clean up," Ahrendts says. "So, for example, we talk about some of the licensees in Japan that we've been closing down. They're profitable, but they're not best for the brand. We've been closing some outlets around the world. They make a lot of money, but [they're] not what's best for the brand. And investors understand that we will continue to grow the revenue and the profits, but we will always clean up as we go during our tenure. We have made this brand as sharp and as pure as we possibly can and are building the great team to do it."

o   Inhale before you exhale; think before you speak.

o   "Actions speak louder than words" is true for everyone — and twice as true for the leader.

o   Speak from your heart, not from your hip. A moment of reflection is the difference between "IQ" and "EQ."

Summary

Communication is not merely telling people what you think and what you know. It is a process in which you seek first to understand what others think.

"We have a great balanced team—on the right, the most creative, and on the left, a great CFO, COO, and the most analytical finance people," Ahrendts says. "We balance the creative and the commercial, the traditional and the digital."

Passionate, confident words motivate. Although information is crucial, if the message lacks inspiration, the team's follow-through may be lackluster—or lacking. As a leader, you must be the message. Without ownership, your words—whether written or spoken—will have little impact. The success of the communication rests in the results it achieves.

CHAPTER 11

LISTEN

*We have two ears and one tongue so
that we would listen more and talk less.*

—*Diogenes*

Years ago, an employee was called into his boss's office. The boss wanted the employee to do well, so he gave him some tough, but crucial, feedback. He told the employee that his inability to connect with people meant that one day his rise would come to an end, because in an evenly matched competition, no one would vouch for him. The boss gave the employee some valuable advice: nobody goes through life being able to pick and choose every person he works with. Rather, he said, leadership is finding those people with whom you really don't want to work or who aren't delivering as much as you do or as much as you would like them to, and somehow getting them to feel some loyalty and fealty to you.

The employee was Ali Velshi, who today is a news anchor and chief business correspondent for CNN.

"I was told that I was such a poor listener that people didn't want to work with me, which was devastating," Velshi recalls.

"My boss told me, 'I want you to succeed, Ali. You need to develop that skill.' He told me something that has stuck with me to this day: he said I had a certain amount of talent—an above-average amount of talent—but that would carry me only so far. That was a turning point in my life and career."

Listening as a leadership skill involves observing with one's eyes and ears, picking up tone, nuance, body language, and eye contact (or lack thereof). Listening detects the texture and the context that happens between the words. When a leader in business, media, or any other field can truly listen, truth emerges.

As one of the most recognizable faces and voices in television news and business journalism today, Velshi knows how to tell a story that will connect with viewers, providing them with information and perspective. His skill, however, is not all talking. In fact, Velshi believes that listening and, in particular, giving people the space to say what is really on their minds

> *If you wish to know the mind of a man, listen to his words.*
>
> —Johann Wolfgang von Goethe

and in their hearts is the key to news reporting—and leadership. As he explains, "When I listen successfully, I get far more out of my interviews or my conversations."

Listening Is Connecting

Listening connects the speaker and the listener emotionally. Beyond the content of the words, a connection is forged through listening and observing, based on the emotions that are conveyed through tone of voice, body language, and facial expression. We know that listening taps into our feelings in a uniquely powerful way. Pounding rainfall, a dentist's drill, a police siren—each elicits a strong emotional response. Or think of how we feel when a familiar tune comes on the radio, and suddenly we're back in some experience, whether it's the high school prom, the first dance at our wedding, or another fond or poignant moment. Now, imagine the connection that can be established when we truly listen to someone else, allowing ourselves to take in the meaning and the emotion of what is being said. Listening is not just hearing the words; it's also paying attention to the nonverbal cues to see how the person is feeling and what she might be thinking.

> Listening is to hearing as speaking is to talking.

"I am a big believer in making a connection with people," Velshi says. "It makes a huge difference. There are people whom I've wanted to interview over the years and who just haven't been comfortable. I have made it a point to go out and meet them or talk to them on the phone ahead of time—to have a conversation with them, even a little bit off topic. I may be a CNN anchor, but nobody owes me anything. If they don't want to talk to me, they are not going to talk to me. They have got to trust that I actually care about what they have to say more than I care about my story or what I think they are going to say."

Listening is to hearing as speaking is to talking. Listening is your monitoring system to discover what's really going on.

You're never going to get emotions from a spreadsheet or body language from a report. Listening is a skill that must be learned and refined. It takes diligent practice. It's not just hearing the words, but also recognizing how they're said. Velshi's description of how he has to get out there and talk to people and not limit himself in any way is analogous to what a CEO has to do. A leader can learn only so much from looking at spreadsheets—he has to get out there with people, because being out there shapes the leader's views.

> Listening is a skill that must be learned and refined.

"When most people think about my job, they assume it's about talking," Velshi says. "But in fact, the talking part of my job is probably the smallest part. I listen to people. When I have conversations with people—talking and listening—it gives me insights that I can't get by reading. I can glean only so much from analysts' reports and from earnings statements. Talking to these constituents gives me a human component that informs my viewers, whether I am talking about companies or stocks or politicians or opportunities. Today, we have more than enough sources of information out there. No one needs to hear me just rehashing what they can find on the Internet. I have got to give them something else. I need an edge in telling a story. By talking to people, engaging people, and listening to people, I catch an implication or a tone or something I would otherwise miss by just reading."

Velshi interviews the powerful, the famous, the influential, and the inspiring. His guests have ranged from Maya

Angelou, the celebrated poet and civil rights activist, to Ford Motor Company CEO Alan Mulally. He spoke with Haitian Prime Minister Jean-Max Bellerive, Coca-Cola CEO Muhtar Kent, and Inter-American Development Bank President Luis Alberto Moreno in their first television interview together about Operation Haiti Hope. Velshi also travels the country, gathering opinions and talking to people "off the beaten media track," as he puts it, giving his reporting an air of authenticity and inclusion.

"One of the things I do is engage my viewership when they are critical of what I do," Velshi says. "I don't simply take all criticism as constructive—I tell people when I think they are wrong. Now that said, I so much appreciate the criticism I receive that every week I do a podcast where I highlight my biggest critics. What I will often do is highlight the back-and-forth that I had with this particular person or read on my podcast what people have said about me and how we performed. I don't like people telling me that I am stupid or that I didn't do a good job, but I am keeping myself honest by not just reading it or listening to it, but being open to it."

Velshi wears two hats at CNN as chief business correspondent and a daily anchor. He groups the people he interviews into three categories. One is broadly accepted leaders, whether they are business leaders, political leaders, or union leaders—people who hold positions of authority in society. A second category is those who don't hold the title of leader, but who are influencers—inventors and creators and people who run organizations and who do things to change the world. The third category is made up of regular, everyday people, whom he considers to be his "clients."

"They are the people I do my job for," Velshi says. "I make a real point of getting out to speak to the people whom I serve in different ways. First, I use social media very actively—that way, I know

> *You cannot truly listen to anyone and do anything else at the same time.*
> —M. Scott Peck

what they are thinking, and I can respond to that very quickly. Second, I go out as much as I can to universities or to other events where I am a speaker, and I take questions. Third, I make a point of traveling around the country and stopping in places the media doesn't stop in, that sometimes even politicians don't stop in—places where people are a little surprised to see me—to get a sense of whether they are getting what they need from me. I have these three constituencies, and I interview and listen to all of them."

Listening to Velshi, it's clear that any leader would similarly benefit from having "journalistic ears."

o   Communication is 80 percent listening and inquiring, and 20 percent speaking. The former must guide the latter.
o   Don't simply hear, listen.
o   Stay focused. Where your eyes go, your attention follows.

Talking More than Listening Closes Your Ears—and Your Mind

Listening requires a singular focus, not just to hear another person, but also to understand her insight, point of view, and emotion. It is the antithesis of multitasking. It is old school. You can't simultaneously read a gadget and genuinely engage with another person. You have to look into the person's eyes to see what words alone cannot convey.

> Communication is 80 percent listening and inquiring, and 20 percent speaking. The former must guide the latter.

In an increasingly visually connected world, listening is a forgotten art. When I was growing up in Kansas, we had three TV stations and a radio station; this was our connection to the outside world. My grandmother loved basketball, particularly the Wichita State Shockers basketball team. I can vividly remember listening intently with my grandmother to games on the radio after supper. The announcers brought the action to us through words and emotion. All around us was an ordinary kitchen, but it felt as if we were there. In our minds, we could see the players driving, getting fouled, or shooting free throws. I could "see" it because of the vivid descriptions that the announcers gave. We were engrossed in the moment because we had no choice but to hear—and to listen.

In our interactions today, listening is a conscious choice that we must make. When we listen, we move away from the back-and-forth of chatter to a quieter, almost reverent space where thoughts are fully formed and expressed. Listening allows for thought-provoking questions and deeper answers in response. It is an invitation: Tell me more. I'm listening. What you have to say is important to me.

"Everybody has a story, and that story may be of remarkable value," Velshi says. "I know that by listening, I give the other person permission to say things that otherwise he or she may not say, whether it's the politician who is guarded, the company CEO who has his talking points, or even the person in Paducah, Kentucky, who is suspicious of the media, and in particular East Coast or 'big city' media."

Although it is highly important, listening may be one of the most undervalued elements of leadership because we take it for granted, mistaking it for the physical capability of hearing. To listen is to be disciplined. No wonder "you never listen to me" is the number one complaint raised in most relationships and in most employee performance reviews. It's even a staple of comedy routines. A friend of mine was raised in a large family in which dinnertime was loud and confusing, with multiple conversations going on at once. People talked over one another, and most of the time no one was actually really listening. My friend's husband came from a smaller and quieter family. For him, it was not uncommon for meals to be eaten in deafening silence. The first time he had dinner with his wife's family, he couldn't believe his ears! "Nobody's listening," he complained.

"That's true," his wife told him, "but if we don't all talk at once, we won't get a chance to say anything. If we waited for everyone to speak, we'd be at the dinner table all night!"

> Listen to educate your intuition.

The problem is that listening takes patience, attention, and time. In addition, human beings are emotional creatures.

They love to share and talk. Many people simply don't want to stop talking. As soon as someone takes a breath, they are ready to jump right in. More than four decades ago, Abraham Kaplan, professor of philosophy at the University of Michigan, coined a term that said it all: "duologues."[1]

> Courage is what it takes to stand up and speak; courage is also what it takes to sit down and listen.
>
> —Winston Churchill

But what if, instead of rushing to speak in a duologue, we allow the silence. Admittedly, this was a challenge for me in the past, when communication always meant talking. Over the years, I have developed the discipline of listening, which has sharpened my observations about others—what they say and how they say it.

When I sat down one day for a conversation with a well-respected leader, I was amazed at how quickly our exchange turned into a monologue. At one point, this leader talked non-stop for 20 minutes. Rather than being offended, I was fascinated that he could talk so much without even a pause. Clearly, he was used to doing all the talking. The experience was a powerful reminder not to let myself become caught up in the same dynamic.

As a leader, you have so much to say and so little time to say it. Although it would seem easier just to download information quickly and efficiently, the lack of listening completely undermines your interaction with others. People feel undervalued, as if their opinions and reactions do not matter, and all because the leader forgot (or refused) to pause and listen.

- Listening puts you in the moment—communicating without saying a word to convey your care, focus, commitment, and understanding.
- Listen, learn, and then lead—in that order.
- Listen to create a culture of candor.

Make It Safe for Others to Tell You the Truth

Listening is a skill, a discipline that is developed over time. It establishes trust in people and makes them feel that it is safe for them to tell you the truth. When followers view the leader first and foremost as a function and second as a person, there are many implications. People will be hesitant or guarded, information will be filtered or managed, and there will be a bias toward the "good news." After all, nobody wants to be the bearer of bad news in any situation—and especially not when it comes to "the boss." The remedy? First, don't be naïve. These tendencies will never be fully eliminated. But you can make it safe for people to tell you the truth. People need to speak without fear of retribution—to be assured that's what's said here, stays here.

> *Listen to the sound of silence.*
>
> —*Paul Simon*

In order to hear the truth, you need to open your ears, your mind, and your office door. Unless you are self-aware, however, the message you're sending may be that you aren't approachable, and this may actually make people believe that you don't want to know what they think. "John" had the best of intentions. He simply valued time for quiet and focus, during which he would not be disturbed. To guard against interruptions, John made a bright red stop sign that he could post outside his office door. That way, people would know when not to knock and break his concentration, and they would also know when it was OK to come in and talk with him.

What was he thinking? Although there was no intended maliciousness, the stop sign offended his direct reports. They perceived him as unapproachable even when his door was open and the sign was taken down. When John found out about their reaction, he was stunned. His only intention, he told everyone, had been to create some solitude so that he could think and work. After taking down the sign, he apologized and assured his team members that he really did want to hear from them. Regaining their trust, however, took time. When a leader puts up a barrier of any kind, communication breaks down. To be an effective leader means to have an open-door policy to listen.

o   If you want the truth, welcome it. This goes for both bad news and differing opinions.

o   Listen to what you don't want to hear. Feedback that is critical or negative is the gift that leaders don't receive enough.

o   Don't close your door (literally) if you say your door is always open.

o   Spare the rod and save the messenger. It takes courage to tell the leader what nobody else will say.

Listen to and through the Silences

As humans, we're programmed to lead with our eyes. Before someone says one word, we have already made snap judgments about that person. Through inquiring and listening, however, we widen the doorway to allow reality to support (or counter) our initial perception and bias. We allow ourselves to experience the other person: not only what he has to say, but, just as important, how he says it.

> Listen, learn, and then lead——in that order.

Listening requires both patience and time. It means creating pauses by exploring, but not scrutinizing. Ask thoughtful questions, and be comfortable with the silences that follow; do not rush to fill the gaps. It may take time and practice, but this skill is one of the most effective in leadership communication. Ask a question—particularly a weighty one—and then let it hang in the air for a moment. If the person doesn't answer right away, wait. Don't rush to explain, soften the tone, or suggest an answer. Allow the other person to process the question and then respond. Your willingness to pause and listen tells the person that this question is very important to you and that her answer is worth waiting for.

"Growing up, I felt compelled to fill the empty space whenever there was a conversation," Velshi says. "When I started spending more time around people like me who did the same things that I did, I realized how unappealing that is."

Listening is not a passive activity. It's high-contact engagement in the here and now, revealing interest, showing understanding, and asking questions. Both the listener and the speaker welcome the pauses that punctuate meaningful conversations, the silences that allow the other person to take a breath and go to the next level, to what has been unspoken until now—the fear, the hope, the plan, the idea, the feedback. This is what you want to hear. This is what you need to know. Before your mind races to say the next word, listen.

"When I was young, my grandmother who brought me up used to say to me, 'Talk less and people may assume that you know more than you do,'" Velshi says. "Now, I think she was a polite woman. What I think she meant to say was, 'Talk less and you are less likely to expose how little you do know.'"

> *When people talk, listen completely. Most people never listen.*
>
> *—Ernest Hemingway*

As he became a better listener, Velshi explains, he began to put himself in the place of the other person. "That means being conscious of what that other person is experiencing with me. What do you see me as? Who am I to you? If I express my displeasure in what you do, do you somehow think that your job is in jeopardy? Does it affect your self-esteem? Do you go and cry (I understood that I had made people cry, which I didn't know)? What is it about what I said that seems so normal to me, but is hurtful or offensive or insulting to somebody else? This is not meant to be solipsistic. I think I had been a solipsistic person before: if I felt hot, it must have been hot, and if I felt hungry, then people must be hungry. I started to learn that it's not just about me. I am one perspective in every discussion. I don't get two votes, just one."

Use questions to explore ideas and to go deeper, but never to attack. Invite the feedback that you want to hear. *Why do you think that happened? What was the problem that caused the delay? What were people seeing that no one wanted to tell anyone about?* If your tone is inquisitive, but not challenging, then you will gain a deeper comprehension. You may be rewarded for your efforts with the most valuable feedback of all — the uncomfortable truth.

○ Listening is discovering what hasn't been said before — what people really think, feel, and believe.

○ Listening is not hearing; it is comprehension of what is said.

○ Listen to educate your intuition.

Listen First, Solve Second

You know what your voice sounds like — and you know what you are thinking. Why limit yourself? You have anchored the organization in the destination, the common purpose, but there are multiple paths for getting there. The purpose of listening is to check the road you are traveling firsthand. It is not to convey your thoughts immediately. There will be a time and a place for that. Rather, seek out the views and recommendations of others from across the organization.

Consider the story about the management of a large luxury hotel that was worried about how it could renovate the property and install another elevator without closing down for weeks and losing revenue. One of the custodians suggested building an elevator outside the hotel. The architects looked into it and decided that it would work. Later, this type of elevator became a standard feature in hotel design. As the story illustrates, you never know where the next innovative solution will come from that might change your organization.

> If you want the truth, welcome the truth.

"I also seek out people who are inspirational—regular people who do extraordinary things to help the world," Velshi says. "I interview people who are unheralded. They are very, very influential to me. There are really a number of people who do what they do without any following, without any church or pulpit, any political party or business or stage of any sort. They do it just because it's the right thing to do. And I have to tell you, we are surrounded by far more of these people than I ever thought. They are just everywhere. They are dedicating their lives and their resources and their money to making the lives of other people better and changing the way things are done. I find that fascinating because if you just listen to the news, you would think we live in a crappy place with nasty people."

Listen to those who are closest to the front line—to your customers, vendors, and strategic partners. Listening to your team empowers others to become part of the "solutions business."

Corporate America can take a lot of lessons from its failings during the Great Recession, especially the "Wall Street vs. Main Street" mentality that resulted partly from the failure of certain executives to listen to what was going on around them.

The perception is that Corporate America failed workers and shareholders. Politicians failed America. Regulators failed from an investment perspective.

> *It is the province of knowledge to speak, and it is the privilege of wisdom to listen.*
>
> *—Oliver Wendell Holmes*

"The tone deafness of business leaders during the financial crisis was staggering to me," Velshi says. "The fact that so many of them just didn't get it. There have been isolated examples of CEOs who just didn't have any sense of why people might be outraged about their compensation. I've never been one of those guys who think compensation needs to be limited, but I am just fascinated by people who don't get why there is a controversy about it, that they're getting 20 or 30 million dollars and they don't understand why someone might be troubled that the economic system is collapsing and people are losing jobs.

"There came to be a mentality out there that, 'Everybody on whom I had come to depend has failed me.' To them, the best thing to do was to adopt a siege mentality or a caveman mentality and say, 'I can spend my money better than the government can; I can do all of these things better for my family and my community than others can.' That's really not a good way to look at the world. Companies that have been successful are those that have been able to send a message that says, 'You can depend on us; you can trust us.' I think corporate America still has some trust to rebuild."

Before companies can put forth their messages, however, they first need to listen to what their key constituencies—their customers and their employees—are saying.

o   Listen without judgment.

o   Listen *for* opportunities, not only *to* problems.

o   Listen to the ideas; be wary of prejudging the messenger.

o   The distance between hearing and listening is thinking and understanding.

Summary

Leadership can be lonely, but it shouldn't be isolating. It is gravitational for communication to cascade down, but it is far harder for it to bubble up. As a leader, you must create freedom of speech through an information-sharing culture. This happens not only through tone, but, more important, through the actions at the top that make listening and inquiring the norm, the routine.

Listening is more than hearing, and it is definitely not just waiting for the other person to take a breath so that you can speak again. Listening is observing and absorbing. By listening, you honor the other person by giving him your full attention. The message you broadcast is that no one is more important to you at that moment.

As the old adage goes, you were given two ears and one mouth for a reason. Make it a genuine reason.

CHAPTER 12

LEARN

*Leadership and learning are
indispensable to each other.*
—*John F. Kennedy*

To be an effective leader, you must have and demonstrate learning agility—the ability to learn from experience and to apply that learning to new or first-time situations. Different from intelligence or simply being smart, learning agility is so important that it is considered a predictor of success.[1] And no wonder. A leader with learning agility excels at absorbing information from his experiences and applying it to the present, and, just as important, creating an agile organization that also learns, grows, and adapts.

At Korn/Ferry, we say that leadership is knowing what to do when you don't know what to do. As a leader, you are voyaging a long way from shore, navigating blue ocean. When you are in uncharted waters, without the benefit of prior knowledge—yours or someone else's—you have to rely on your learning agility to be your inner compass. All you can do is extrapolate from your past learning and prior experience to solve problems and challenges that you've never encountered before.

When Mark Thompson first joined the BBC as a 22-year-old production trainee, he brought with him an insatiable curiosity about the world. He chose to carry out his pursuit of information and his sharing of knowledge and ideas through the British Broadcasting Corporation (BBC), one of the preeminent public broadcasting organizations in the world. Today, he is director-general of the BBC, the culmination of a professional lifetime spent in a world of media that has expanded far beyond the traditional broadcast venues of radio and television to embrace a digital, online world. As the leader of a global news organization, he oversees 23,000 employees around the world, from metropolitan newsrooms to the front lines of geopolitical tensions.

> What you knew yesterday, got you where you are today. What you learn today determines your success tomorrow.

Over the years, Thompson's purpose has not changed. Since his earliest days with the BBC, he has sought to demonstrate its relevance. As he observed, "When I joined the BBC, I believed in the values of the organization: best journalism in the world; arts, history, and science available to every household." Today, he faces the same challenge: proving the relevance of the BBC, but in a world that's vastly different, especially when it comes to technology, from the world of 1979 when Thompson first joined the organization.

"Broadcast media began with very specialized, professional technology whose workings were understood only by highly trained specialists and engineers," Thompson explains. "Equipment was expensive. The engineers and technicians were of a different tribe from the content people, who were the arts graduates wearing tweed jackets and the female equivalent and who were thinking about the great ideas of the comedies and dramas. Today, more consumers have access to sophisticated equipment. You can shoot a feature film with an iPhone—that's part of a broader democratizing and spreading of technology to the people who used to be consumers. Second, the difference between content creativity and science/engineering creativity is breaking down. Video games are an example, as are websites. Creative innovation often happens in the boundary between technology and content."

Thompson's world is one in which leadership means learning—and also teaching and informing. Thus, he exemplifies an important aspect of a leader's role: to expand what one knows and to empower others through the sharing of knowledge. Leaders today must also be savvy when it comes to utilizing new and emerging technologies to connect, communicate, and collaborate. With the help of technology—the Internet, intranets, social media, Webinars, and more—information flows like water, without resistance.

In Thompson's world, technology and information affect the way the news stories are told. A powerful example is the media coverage of the devastating March 2011 earthquake and tsunami in Japan, where major news organizations used clips from amateur videos that captured what was happening in the moment to inform viewers. Where emotion is involved, learning intensifies. In the same general time frame, there appeared to be a noticeably significant rise in the amount of amateur video footage coming out of the Middle East, from the protests in the aftermath of the Iran election to the uprisings in Tunisia, Egypt, Yemen, Libya, and Bahrain. With access restricted in some cases for traditional news-gathering organizations like the BBC, video being shared on social websites by the protestors themselves became an important way that images reached the rest of the world. Professional journalists and organizations such as the BBC integrated amateur video footage into their coverage to enrich their reports. "In this world, there has never been a better time for user-generated content," Thompson says. "We certainly saw that during the earthquake and the tsunami. At the same time, the world is jammed with media and choices. People whose knowledge and judgment you trust are at a premium."

> It's not failure, it's called learning.

Although citizen video journalism is not new and has long been used by news organizations for incidents ranging from plane crashes to wars and natural disasters, mobile devices and social networking video sites such as YouTube have resulted in a dramatic increase in the amount of content available, the speed of delivery, the ability to deliver outside of normal controls, and the viral way in which content can spread around the globe. That, in turn, has challenged traditional news organizations to change course—quite drastically in many instances. It's up to leaders like Thompson to not abandon their previous strategies, but to be constantly learning about the various platforms across which people are consuming media, and to incorporate the new tools and methods that technological advances make possible.

"The lesson of the digital age, which is true for media and technology, is, if you get behind the curve, it's hard to catch up again," Thompson says. "Getting too far in front of the curve is dangerous as well. Pace of change and timing are really important."

> Knowledge is what you know. Wisdom is acknowledging what you don't know.

Using the broadcast industry as an example, Thompson recalls that three years ago, no one felt that mobile TV or TV on mobile devices would ever be a threat. The only place it would be appealing, according to the consensus at the time, was in Japan, where many consumers have very long commutes. Now, in the age of iPhones and iPads, British consumers are lapping up mobile TV. "They are sitting up in bed, watching TV on an iPad. They love TV on mobile devices. The BBC and the country need a plan for how to get broadcast TV to these devices [because] we've seen behaviors [among consumers] over the last 12 to 15 months that we weren't expecting. We have to change our strategies as a result," Thompson says.

To face these types of changes—particularly as technology opens new doors and also allows new competitive entrants—leaders must continually learn. Clinging to the past and pretending that the status quo will never change is the road to extinction. Learning and remaining open to new ways is the path to distinction.

As a learning leader, Thompson has taken on challenges brought about by everything from technology to geopolitics, and the occasional controversy as well. He has learned to lead by putting himself in new and sometimes uncomfortable situations, and in areas in which he had to develop expertise quickly. Although he celebrates learning as a highly valued leadership skill, Thompson recognizes that there is no alternative. Not to learn is to stay rooted in the past. In any organization, but especially one as fast-paced, competitive, and technology-sensitive as media, unwillingness to learn is a fatal flaw.

"One of the characteristics of a lot of the leaders I most admire, and that I like to think is true of me as well, is having a voracious appetite for learning. The willingness to learn is as important as anything you can learn along the way," Thompson says. "One interesting differentiator of potential leaders is whether their appetite to learn continues or maybe even grows throughout their careers, or diminishes and eventually comes to an end. One of the main reasons that people don't progress in their careers in an organization like the BBC is they, in essence, become satisfied with the level of knowledge and skills they've got."

> *All truths are easy to understand once they are discovered; the point is to discover them.*
> —*Galileo Galilei*

Leadership starts with capability, which over time is developed into competence. Simply stated, you have to know what you are doing. But that's just the beginning. It also entails working smarter by getting smarter through continuous If you stagnate as a leader, you will impede the organization's progress—and put an end to your leadership.

The More You Know, the More You See What You Don't Know

Knowledge is what you know. Wisdom is acknowledging what you don't know. Learning and discernment are the bridge between the two.

At the BBC, a rich legacy from the past and an insatiable curiosity about the future come together in an interesting mission to educate and inspire. "At the BBC, we are passionate curators, from the classic museum to an unsigned pop band," Thompson says. "We are professionals who are in love with the arts, culture, or entertainment—or history, science, and news. That is an interesting position to be in." The same can be said for every organization—and, in fact, for every leader. Perspective comes from remembering the past, but not staying there. Executing in the present leads to a successful future.

> *Real knowledge is to know the extent of one's ignorance.*
>
> —*Confucius*

"Over the years, I've had many colleagues from whom I've learned," Thompson says. "I also think it's very useful to have fairly regular critical appraisals. Even now, a couple of times a year, I have a structured conversation with my boss, who is the chair of the BBC's governing body, about what went well, what didn't, what are the things for me to think about, maybe issues that I should have discussed with the governing body. There is no reason why the chief executive shouldn't have performance appraisals, with all the lessons learned and development points written down for follow-up, just like anyone else in the organization."

o   What got you here won't get you there. Adapt and adopt.
o   Let your curiosity lead you. Commit to continuously learning—for yourself and for your team.
o   Distill complexity into simplicity.

Leaders Do Not Have the Luxury of Not Knowing

When you are a leader, people look to you not only for the vision forward, but for the assurance that the team will get there. Leaders are builders of confidence. Therefore, you do not have the luxury of shrugging your shoulders and saying you don't know. As a leader, you will not have all the answers, but you must know where to find them quickly by surrounding yourself with diversity in thought.

"In the last decade, I've had to learn more about technology than in the whole rest of my life," Thompson says. "It's not good enough for the chief executive of a big media company not to have a basic grounding in technology—the way in which information is handled and distributed and manipulated and so forth. I've had to do a great deal of learning. One of the most basic and obvious points is, if you don't understand something, you should ask people to explain to you what it is they're talking about, what a particular term means. Don't be ashamed of not knowing things. There is no reason why someone who hasn't got a computer science degree should understand every aspect of how Adobe Flash works, or what a run time is, or the particular issues of trans-coding digital media. If you don't understand, ask."

The more you stretch, the more you learn. Rather than relying totally on the knowledge of others, become conversant in a new area. For example, as the leader, you do not need to have technology expertise that's on a par with that of your technologists. However, you need to be able to communicate with them. Otherwise, how will you understand the problems and solutions that they bring to your attention?

No matter how high you rise, or how much you accomplish, be a continuous learner.

In 1986, 48-year-old John Corcoran drove to the adult learning center of his local public library in Carlsbad City, California, in search of what had eluded him all his life: the ability to read. Although he was a college graduate and a successful businessman, Corcoran had gone through life with virtually no literacy skills. The improvisation and even deception he had had to rely on to conceal his inability to read are unfathomable. No matter what he was able to accomplish materially, however, Corcoran never could fill the void of having been the young boy in the "dumb row" in elementary school who had not been taught to read.

> *Experience: that most brutal of teachers. But you learn, my God do you learn.*
>
> —*C. S. Lewis*

Finally, after 13 months of one-on-one tutoring, Corcoran achieved a sixth-grade reading level. Later diagnosed as having a severe auditory discrimination problem, Corcoran received intensive instruction and finally achieved the breakthrough of reading on a twelfth-grade level.

A nationally known literacy advocate, Corcoran became the first adult learner to serve on the National Institute for Literacy, appointed by President George H. W. Bush and confirmed for an additional term by President Bill Clinton. A lifelong learner, he turned his personal adversity into advocacy for others—and all because he never gave up on his quest to learn how to read.[2]

The day you stop learning is the day you start dying.

o   Don't pretend to know things that you don't know. Have a plan to learn what you need to know before you need to know it.

o   Visualize the end state before you begin.

o   Leaders are not expected to be experts in everything, but they must be in the solutions business.

Success Breeds Confidence, but Failure Leads to Wisdom

Every leader must be reconciled to the fact that failure is inevitable, while at the same time truly believing that every attempt will be a success. Leaders do not allow the team to become paralyzed by setbacks. Leadership means reshaping the occasional defeat into momentum by learning from the cause of failure and correcting one's course to ensure future success.

"I've definitely learned over the years that leadership is a conversation, which involves shutting up and listening as well as speaking," Thompson says. "It's something that quite a few people in management forget or never learn. With most solutions that you're searching for, someone in the organization has the answer or part of the answer. That means listening, allowing the debate, and sometimes letting colleagues prove you wrong. That's healthy. It's not a sign of weakness; it's actually a strength. It takes real confidence to say, 'Maybe you're right and I'm not. Thank you.' If as a leader you're in transmit-only mode—giving out opinions, orders, and instructions—fairly soon, you'll be the only person in the room."

In the laboratory as in life, more experimentation leads to more chances to do something better, instead of doing things the same way, yet expecting a different outcome. Trial and error eventually produce improvements and breakthroughs. Innovation can come only from teams that are curious, like to experiment, and can deal with change effectively. Where there is a passion for ideas, there is fertile ground for creativity.

One day a farmer's donkey fell into a well. The farmer frantically thought about what he could do as the stricken animal cried out to be rescued. With no obvious solution, the farmer regretfully concluded that because the donkey was old and the well needed to be filled in anyway, he should give up the idea of rescuing the beast. Instead, he should simply fill in the well. Hopefully the poor animal would not suffer too much, he tried to persuade himself.

An investment in knowledge pays the best interest.

—Benjamin Franklin

The farmer asked his neighbors for help, and before long, they all began to shovel earth quickly into the well. When the donkey realized what was happening, he wailed and struggled, but then, to everyone's relief, the noise stopped.

After a while, the farmer looked down into the well and was astonished by what he saw. The donkey was still alive and was progressing toward the top of the well. He had learned that by shaking off the dirt instead of letting it cover him, he could step on the accumulating soil as the level rose. When the donkey reached the top of the well, he stepped over the edge and gave the farmer one last look. "Now who's the jackass?" the donkey remarked, and trotted happily away.

Learning is all about adapting, being open-minded, and being willing to find solutions that aren't obvious.

o   Orient yourself toward newness and creativity. You can't learn from things you aren't doing.

o   Don't blame—learn.

o   The only real failure is failing to fail—which means you are either oblivious or too cautious.

Improve Yourself to Improve the Organization

By nature, leaders should be curious, captivated, and engaged. They must be self-aware and comfortable with who they are as people, which extends far beyond what they do. Being a leader is more about who you are than it is about what you do.

As a leader, you must be a critical thinker, able to handle complexity and ambiguity. Elevate your leadership, and your followers will respond. The more you learn, the more you will improve, and you will bring the organization along with you.

"In my world, the media world, you start off by learning how to make decisions about things: What are we going to lead the news with today? How are we going to do this TV interview? And you progressively end up making decisions about people," Thompson says. "Something that comes from experience and from making mistakes is the way in which you think about and relate to people."

He shares the story of how for many years his job was being a commissioner of TV—running a TV channel, both for the BBC and also as a TV executive for channel 4. The responsibilities of the job appeared to be largely to find programming to fill the schedule. But, as Thompson discovered, it was really more about finding and trusting people than it was about choosing ideas. "After a while," he says, "what really matters is finding the right people."

> *It's what you learn after you know it all that counts.*
> —John Wooden

For all leaders, a powerful lesson to learn is how to find and develop the right people, not mere replicas of the leader. Leaders must be comfortable with differing views, providing others with the opportunity to dissent.

As a leader, you must always solicit recommendations and solutions from the members of your team. Hear the opinions of your team members, and, if they can convince you to see things differently, be willing to change your mind.

"You learn over time that it's very important that people genuinely tell you their ideas and have the freedom to tell you what they want to do," Thompson says. "So instead of listening to somebody pitching you the program that he thinks you want to hear about, you learn that you have to give [people] enough space to pitch the programs that they care most passionately about: 'I believe in this program . . . I believe in this service or piece of functionality because . . .' Often, in those sorts of situations, you're trying to simplify the relationship and get to a point of absolute clarity and honesty about what's going on. Which of the 10 ideas just presented does the person really want to create? The message to the person is, tell me why you are excited and maybe I'll get excited, too."

o   Never stop looking in the mirror—be a continuous learner.

o   Achievements fade, but progress inspires and learning endures.

o   It's not simply what you've done, but also what you've learned.

Summary

The distance between your organization and its competition is not absolute. As a leader, you must outgrow your organization in order to fuel its growth, enabling it to create greater separation from the best of the rest. Surround yourself with a handful of people who will be your corrective lens, making sure that you focus and learn. Equally important, your inner circle should be made up of confidants who provide grounding and perspective, seeing you as a person rather than a function.

"Learning is about accretion of knowledge and expertise; of course that's part of it," Thompson says. "But also it's a way of getting a sense of what the real levers of change are. What are the real dynamics and the real drivers of values, and the real pitfalls and what could go wrong?"

Your willingness to keep learning makes a powerful statement to the entire organization: the bar is being raised ever higher. You will learn far more lessons when mistakes are made

> The only real failure is failing to fail.

than when success comes easily. These tough lessons will prepare you for a future that is highly competitive, in which the new and the creative are not only desired, but expected. Your ability to learn and adapt will determine your fate and that of many others.

"Your ability to learn about and to learn from people goes on and, in some ways, gets deeper," Thompson says. "I don't feel it diminishing in me. But other people certainly claim that they feel less comfortable learning about other areas of knowledge or disciplines."

Leaders also have a heightened realization that no one is invincible or irreplaceable. They recognize their own professional mortality; at some point, they will step aside, either voluntarily or involuntarily. As observed earlier, you must never lose sight of your responsibility to be a steward of the organization. One day, you will leave. When you do, the organization must be in a substantially better place than it was before you inherited it.

In the meantime, distinguish your leadership not only by what you know, but also by your open and curious mind. If knowledge is power, then empower yourself and everyone around you to know, do, and be more.

Learning never ends.

EPILOGUE
It's All About the People...

n the end, it's not really about the products made, the technology developed, or the financial instruments that are bought and sold. It's all about the people. Yes, a leader must have deep capabilities in the "solutions business," charting a course around and through the obstacles ahead to reach the desired goals. Leaders must learn from failure, thrive on competition, work hard, and radiate hope. They are flexible, adaptable, and open to feedback, while believing so strongly in the journey that they remain determined and confident, and cannot be derailed by idle criticism.

Yet, as I know in my role as CEO of Korn/Ferry International, and from my travels to meet with leaders around the world, a singular truth remains: to be a leader is to be in the "people business." No matter what technical competencies are required in their current circumstances, whether to launch a startup or engineer a turnaround, the people part of leadership is the singular, foundational principle. It means connecting and aligning the rough and sometimes jagged edges of individuality into a smooth and seamless mosaic.

From Bangkok to Baltimore, this basic truth crosses borders and transcends cultures: Leadership requires followership. To create followership, leaders must meet people where they are. To lead is to make an emotional connection on a very real and human level in every interaction. Leaders commit to meeting the needs of those who follow. With grace, dignity, and restraint, effective leaders always focus on the other person. What matters most is not what the leader accomplishes, but what others achieve.

With the possible exception of dictators and tyrants, leaders are not self-proclaimed and self-anointed. As witnessed throughout history, and as we've seen most recently during the Arab Spring political movement, leaders who lack the power of the people will eventually be toppled. In politics and in business, others make the decision of who leads. Leadership is not a unilateral action; it requires others. People vote with their feet. If they do not like where a leader is going, what he stands for, or how he goes about accomplishing his goals, they will leave. That leader may charge up the mountain, but somewhere on the path he will face the painful truth that he is alone. A leader may be the most brilliant strategist, incredibly decisive, well read and reflective, but she cannot go it alone. Otherwise, she is not a leader, only a soloist.

Leaders act as the mirrors for their organizations. What they radiate—whether confidence and optimism, or doubt and confusion—others are going to feel. Leaders must understand the selflessness that leadership demands. The leader journeys with the team, sometimes in front, other times behind, but always with and in the company of others.

How, then, does a leader commit to this journey and engage others—heart, mind, and soul? The answer lies in the Absolutes of Leadership.

Over the course of my more than 25 years in business—as an employee, a manager, and a leader, including as CFO and now CEO of a publicly traded firm—I have learned, applied, and relied on the leadership framework presented in this book. More recently, as a guest lecturer at prestigious institutions of higher learning—including Northwestern University's Kellogg School of Management, one of the premier business schools in the United States, and the China Europe International Business School, one of the top business schools in Asia—I have presented the elements of this framework to those who will effect change in the future. It continues to impress and inspire me how applicable these elements are, whether I'm speaking in Chicago or Shanghai.

Tried and true and battle-tested by time, the absolutes are the building blocks that must be present, regardless of one's leadership style or approach. They are the result of a lifetime commitment to define my own leadership, building on my strengths and focusing on my weaknesses, and drawing upon the influence and inspiration of leaders whom I admire. At first glance, these elements may seem simple. It is incredibly difficult, however, to do them completely and consistently. There is far more complexity here than meets the eye. No matter how intuitive they seem, practicing them day in and day out is emotionally taxing.

Just take one aspect, such as making an emotional connection, and apply it every day. Challenge yourself to ensure that in every interaction people feel better after engaging with you, even in difficult discussions, than they did before. You'll see how exhausting it is (although you can't show it). Yet the reward is well worth the effort: the ability to motivate and empower others to become aligned with the purpose and vision of the organization, and in the process to expand themselves to become capable of more than they thought possible.

As you put these elements into practice, you may very well find that some are easier or more natural than others. For example, you may have talent for navigate, yet communicate is more difficult. You understand the importance of strategy, but are inconsistent in your efforts to empower and reward. Avoid the temptation to pick and choose among your own strengths. Focus on your weaknesses to build yourself; as you, the leader, grow so will the organization. The elements cannot be adopted "a la carte"; you can't be "all in all the time" without a complete commitment.

By embracing the Absolutes of Leadership you will become better able to handle the challenges of today and prepare for those of tomorrow. Everywhere you look, people are focused on change—economically, politically, and socially. We believe in change and certainly our enthusiasm is warranted. Over the past 50 years, we have seen more change than in any similar stretch in history. The paradox, however, is that bringing about meaningful change necessitates reliance on things that should not change—values and qualities of leadership that are everlasting and absolute. By focusing on what matters most, we are not deterred or defeated by change, but rather increase our competency to respond and even to initiate it.

The "Peter Principle," which was introduced by Dr. Lawrence Peter and Raymond Hull in their book of the same name, asserts that people rise to their level of incompetence— meaning that they get promoted until they are beyond their capabilities and become ineffective.[1] Kenneth P. De Meuse, a colleague of mine at Korn/Ferry, asserts that today's workplace has created a new principle, one that is even more insidious. He calls it the Paul Principle: Employees do not need to get promoted to become incompetent; that can happen in their current jobs. Why? Because they do not grow, adapt, and evolve as their jobs become more complex, more ambiguous, and more technologically demanding. The same holds true for organizational leaders. Unless leaders continue to learn new competencies and behaviors, they risk going the way of inkwells, 8-tracks, and typewriters.

Successful leaders continue to learn, bend, and flex as their world changes. In other words, they are learning agile. As stated earlier in the book, at Korn/Ferry we believe learning agility has become the No. 1 predictor of leadership success, more accurately than IQ and EQ (emotional intelligence), education level, or even leadership competencies. As a leader expands her knowledge and capabilities, she is better equipped to deliver change by linking the organization's purpose—its reason for being—with people's desire to be part of something bigger than themselves. That is why purpose is the first of the elements, the initial building block upon which all others must be balanced. With purpose defined, the leader can guide the way through strategy, people, measure, empower, and reward—all the while anticipating, navigating, communicating, listening, learning, and ultimately leading.

To lead is to define a common purpose that transcends individual self-interest. What matters most is the organization's shared interest. Achieving this goal requires that people become empowered and inspired to align with a greater purpose and in so doing actualize their own hopes and dreams.

NOTES

Chapter 6

1. D. Michael Abrashoff, *It's Your Ship: Management Techniques from the Best Damn Ship in the Navy* (New York: Warner Books, 2002).

Chapter 7

1. Scientific Management, comprising *Shop Management, The Principles of Scientific Management and Testimony Before the Special House Committee*, by Frederick Winslow Taylor, Harper & Row, 1911.
2. "The Legion Letter," Volume XVIII, No. 1, American Legion Wayne M. Kidwell Post #184

Chapter 8

1. Jon Krakauer. *Into Thin Air: A Personal Account of the Mt. Everest Disaster*. (New York: Anchor Books, 1999).
2. The Wright Brothers, Wilbur and Orville Wright, http://www.wright-house.com/wright-brothers/Wrights.html.

Chapter 9

1. Peter King, "Tom Brady is Back," *Sports Illustrated*, June 1, 2009
2. Andrew Chaikin, "For Neil Armstrong, the First Moon Walker, It Was All about Landing the Eagle," *Scientific American*, July 19, 2009.

Chapter 10

1. Mohamed ElBaradei, "Wael Ghonim: Spokesman for a Revolution," *Time*. April 21, 2011.
2. Congressional Research Service Report #RS21408

Chapter 11

1. "Behavior: The Art of Not Listening," *Time*, January 24, 1969; http://www.time.com/time/magazine/article/0,9171,900576,00. html#ixzz1NJ0mxbL6.

Chapter 12

1. Robert Eichinger, Michael Lombardo, and Cara Carpetta, *FYI For Learning Agility*, (Lominger International, 2004-2010)
2. John Corcoran. *The Bridge to Literacy: No Child - Or Adult - Left Behind.* (New York: Kaplan, 2009)

Epilogue

1. Peter, Lawrence and Hull, Raymond (1969 Rev. 1993), *The Peter Principle: Why Things Go Wrong.* Buccaneer Books.

INDEX

ABOUT THE AUTHOR

Gary Burnison is chief executive officer of Korn/Ferry International, the world's largest executive recruiting firm and a leading global provider of talent management solutions. Based in Los Angeles, the firm delivers an array of solutions that help clients to attract, deploy, develop, and reward their talent. Burnison is a regular contributor to CNBC, CNN, Fox Business, and to other international news outlets. He lives in Los Angeles with his wife, Leslie, and children.